DINNER
SPECIAL

Corn Bread with Scallions,
page 187

DINNER
SPECIAL

185 RECIPES FOR A GREAT MEAL ANY NIGHT OF THE WEEK

FOOD&WINE
BOOKS

Published by Oxmoor House, an imprint of
Time Inc. Books, a division of
Meredith Corporation
225 Liberty Street
New York, NY 10281

SENIOR EDITOR **Betty Wong**

FOOD & WINE BOOKS EDITOR **Anne Cain**

PROJECT EDITOR **Tara Stewart Hardee**

DESIGNER **Alisha Petro**

DESIGN DIRECTOR **Melissa Clark**

PHOTO DIRECTOR **Paden Reich**

PRODUCTION MANAGER **Stephanie Thompson**

ASSISTANT PRODUCTION DIRECTOR
Sue Chodakiewicz

ASSISTANT PRODUCTION MANAGER
Diane Rose Keener

COPY EDITOR **Jacqueline Giovanelli**

PROOFREADER **Donna Baldone**

INDEXER **Mary Ann Laurens**

FELLOW **Holly Ravazzolo**

ISBN-13: 978-0-8487-5612-3
Library of Congress Control Number:
2018934176
First Edition 2018
Printed in the United States of America
10 9 8 7 6 5 4 3 2 1

FOOD & WINE MAGAZINE

EDITOR IN CHIEF **Hunter Lewis**

EXECUTIVE EDITOR **Karen Shimizu**

MANAGING EDITOR **Caitlin Murphee Miller**

EXECUTIVE WINE EDITOR **Ray Isle**

SENIOR FOOD EDITOR **Mary-Frances Heck**

CULINARY DIRECTOR **Justin Chapple**

We welcome your comments and suggestions
about Time Inc. Books.
Time Inc. Books
Attention: Book Editors
P.O. Box 62310
Tampa, Florida 33662-2310

Time Inc. Books products may be purchased
for business or promotional use. For information
on bulk purchases, please contact Christi
Crowley in the Special Sales Department at
(845) 895-9858.

FRONT COVER **Grilled Lamb with Pickled
Eggplant Salad and Herbed Yogurt (page 171)**

BACK COVER **Rustic Sausage and
Three-Cheese Lasagna (page 214)**

PHOTOGRAPHER **Con Poulos**

For additional photo contributors,
see page 254.

AT FOOD & WINE we believe in dinner. For most of us, it's the only time of day we get to spend in the kitchen during the work week and our only chance to sit down at the table to savor a meal with friends and family. Dinner is special. So why does it often feel hurried and unsatisfying? We know from experience that a little inspiration and planning can elevate weeknight dinners. And that's how the concept for the *Dinner Special* cookbook was born.

We've pulled together recipes from outstanding chefs like Hugh Acheson, Lidia Bastianch, Jonathan Waxman, April Bloomfield, and Deborah Schneider and used those recipes to create weeknight-friendly menus featuring a main dish, two side dishes and a wine, beer or cocktail recommendation from our executive wine editor Ray Isle. You can follow the meal plans we've put together, or mix and match your favorite dishes to create your own combinations.

A few notes about the menus: We've organized *Dinner Special* by season, with chapters for spring, summer, fall and winter, because that's how we like to eat. It's hard to beat asparagus in the spring, a grilled tomato salad in the summer, and roasted acorn squash in the fall. That said, feel free to jump around—there's no rule that says you can't enjoy a cool crisp salad in midwinter, and you'll find most of the fruits and vegetables that our recipes call for at the supermarket year-round. Most of the menus serve four but can easily be scaled up for the times you feel like inviting guests for dinner—and of course we've got meals for the holidays as well (See the Holiday Meal Planner at right).

To help make dinner preparation less time-consuming, we've included strategies for stocking your pantry with essential ingredients (page 229), key make-ahead recipes (page 234) and our favorite ways to use leftovers (page 243).

Cheers to you as you make every dinner a special one.

—The Editors

Holiday Meal Planner

Cooking for a special occasion? Check out these 12 festive dinner menus.

VALENTINE'S DAY 221
Meatballs in Tomato Sauce, Romaine and Tomato Salad, Broccoli Rabe with Black Olives

ST. PATRICK'S DAY 58
Slow Cooker Corned Beef, Irish Brown Bread, Steamed Leeks

EASTER 63
Roast Leg of Lamb, Peas with Spring Onions, Steamed New Potatoes

CINCO DE MAYO 85
Chipotle Chicken Tacos, Grilled Vegetables, Chile-and-Mango Guacamole

MOTHER'S DAY 15
Spinach Frittata, Grilled Tomato Crostini, Little Gem Lettuce with Beets

MEMORIAL DAY 97
Sausage Burgers, Grilled Potato Salad, Corn on the Cob

4TH OF JULY 105
Barbecued Baby Back Ribs, Peppered Corn Bread, Grilled Tomato Salad

LABOR DAY 217
Pulled Pork Sandwiches, Crispy Buffalo Potatoes, Red-and-Green Coleslaw

HALLOWEEN 184
Cumin Chili, Jicama Salad, Scallion Corn Bread

THANKSGIVING 163
Thyme-Basted Pork Tenderloin, Roasted Acorn Squash, Spicy Brussels Sprouts

CHRISTMAS 225
Pepper-Crusted Prime Rib, Accordion Potatoes, Creamed Kale

NEW YEAR'S EVE 177
Roasted Brussels Sprouts Quiche, Tangy Apple Salad, Sweet Potato–Squash Gratin

WEEKNIGHT STRATEGIES

Weeknight dinners can sometimes be a challenge. These tips for shopping and stocking your fridge and pantry will help you get dinner on the table with minimal stress.

Do Ahead of Time

COOK UP A BATCH OF GRAINS on Sunday to have available during the week. Try quinoa, farro, wheat berries or bulgur. Boil grains in salted water until al dente, like pasta, then spread them out on a baking sheet to cool. Store them in separate containers in the refrigerator.

WASH AND PREP YOUR FRUITS AND VEGETABLES before you put them away. It makes it quicker to throw together sides or salads later in the week.

FREEZE MEATBALLS WITH SAUCE in plastic bags, then defrost them to make meatball heroes or serve over fresh pasta. You can cook a big batch and the next few meals are a cinch. (See Meatballs in Tomato Sauce on page 221.)

KEEP EXTRA PESTO IN THE FREEZER to use in pasta and soups. Chill it first in an ice bath, top the container with a bit of olive oil, then freeze. Or freeze in ice cube trays wrapped in plastic.

Cut Cooking Time

FRESH VEGETABLES are the key to quick and easy meals, especially in the spring and summer when fresh produce abounds. Try no-cook salads, chilled vegetable soups, sandwiches and veggie stir-fries. (See Golden Gazpacho with Avocado on page 74.)

PASTA is an all-time favorite for simple weeknight suppers and there are many choices for shapes and sizes of pasta as well as sauces. (See Pasta with Asparagus Pesto on page 44 and Andouille Mac & Cheese on page 209.)

SKIRT STEAK is a flavorful cut that's ideal for quick dinners because it grills and broils quickly.

SKINLESS, BONELESS CHICKEN BREASTS OR THIGHS cook in 20 minutes or less and can be used in a wide variety of recipes.

SHRIMP is great when you're pressed for time because it cooks so quickly. Jumbo ones make any dish more hearty and more luxurious.

Shop Smarter

Having a stocked pantry will help you quickly boost flavor in any dish and improvise as inspiration strikes. See page 229 for more of our favorite pantry staples.

Love Your Leftovers

Learn to transform leftovers into genius dishes and you get two meals for the price of one. Turn to page 243 for some innovative ways to use leftovers.

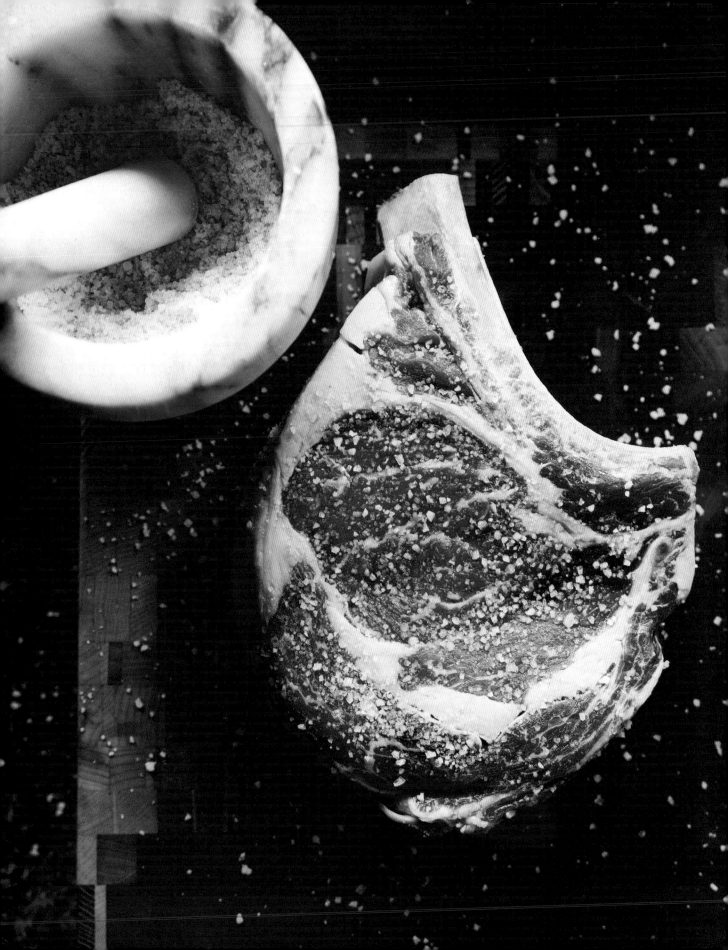

spring

Spinach Frittata   15
+Grilled Tomato Crostini
+Little Gem Lettuce with Beets

Cheese Enchiladas   19
+Skillet Corn and Peppers
+Crudités à la Mexicaine
+BONUS: COCKTAIL
  Margarita

Grilled Tuna   23
+Sweet-and-Sour Green Beans
+Quinoa Pilaf

Tequila-Chipotle Shrimp   27
+Spanish Rice
+Broccolini and Escarole Salad

Fish Tacos   31
+Spicy Pea Guacamole
+Black Bean and Rice Salad

Seared Scallops   35
+Cauliflower Puree
+Spring Vegetable Panzanella

Crab Cakes   40
+Green Beans
+Warm Potato Salad
+BONUS: COCKTAIL
  Gin and Tonic

Salmon Papillotes   43
+Pasta with Asparagus Pesto
+Buttermilk-Dressed Spring Greens

Glazed Chicken Legs   48
+Roasted Broccoli
+Fried Rice

Spring Beef Stew   51
+Buttermilk-Parmesan Biscuits
+Boston Lettuce Salad

Spiced Brown Sugar Ham   55
+Classic Potato Salad
+Sautéed Spring Greens

Slow Cooker Corned Beef   60
+Irish Brown Bread
+Steamed Leeks
+BONUS: COCKTAIL
  Lady Irish

Roast Leg of Lamb   63
+Peas with Spring Onions
+Steamed New Potatoes

Spinach Frittata
+ Grilled Tomato Crostini
+ Little Gem Lettuce with Beets

The combination of flavors in this frittata is pure genius. Tarragon is classic with both spinach and eggs, and a touch of sharp feta cheese accents the trio beautifully. Tara Stevens' modern take on a traditional roasted beet salad features Little Gem lettuce and fresh herbs to complement the frittata, and savory tomato-basil crostini from Melissa Rubel Jacobson rounds out the meal. This fresh spring menu can also do double duty as brunch.

SPINACH, FETA AND TARRAGON FRITTATA
Total 25 min; Serves 4

2 Tbsp. butter

2 scallions including green tops, thinly sliced

10 oz. spinach, stems removed, leaves washed and cut into thin strips

1½ tsp. dried tarragon

¼ tsp. kosher salt, divided

¼ tsp. pepper, divided

8 large eggs

1½ Tbsp. chopped fresh tarragon

1 Tbsp. extra-virgin olive oil

3 oz. feta cheese, crumbled (about ⅓ cup)

1. In a 12-inch nonstick ovenproof skillet, melt 1 tablespoon of the butter over moderate heat. Add the scallions and cook, stirring, for 1 minute. Add the spinach, dried tarragon and ⅛ teaspoon each of salt and pepper. Cook, stirring frequently, until the liquid evaporates, about 3 minutes. Transfer the spinach mixture to a bowl and let cool. Wipe out the skillet.

2. In a large bowl, beat the eggs with the remaining ⅛ teaspoon each of salt and pepper. Stir in the spinach mixture and fresh tarragon.

3. Preheat the broiler and position a rack 6 inches from the heat. In the skillet, melt the remaining 1 tablespoon of butter with the 1 tablespoon of oil over moderate heat. Pour in the egg mixture and reduce the heat to low. Sprinkle the feta on top and cook until the bottom is golden brown and the top is almost set, 6 to 7 minutes. Transfer the skillet to the broiler and broil the frittata until the eggs are set, 2 to 3 minutes.

4. Using a spatula, lift up the edge of the frittata and slide it onto a plate. Cut into wedges and serve.

NOTE If the handle of your skillet isn't ovenproof, protect it from the heat of the broiler by wrapping it with about four layers of aluminum foil.

DIY Dried Herbs

F&W's Justin Chapple hates letting his fresh herb crop go to waste, so he dries fresh sprigs quickly in the microwave to extend their shelf life. The most zappable herbs are sturdy ones like rosemary, thyme and oregano.

STEP 1 Arrange sprigs of fresh herbs on a paper towel so they don't touch each other.

STEP 2 Microwave at high power in 20-second bursts until the herbs are dried and crisp; turn and flip them between intervals.

STEP 3 Run your fingers along the sprigs to strip off leaves. Discard stems and store the dried herbs in spice jars.

3. Using scissors, carefully cut open the foil packets. Spoon the tomatoes and their juices over the grilled bread and drizzle with olive oil. Sprinkle with salt and basil and serve. —*Melissa Rubel Jacobson*

LITTLE GEM LETTUCE WITH ROASTED BEETS AND FETA DRESSING

Active 20 min; Total 1 hr 20 min; Serves 4

1 Tbsp. cumin seeds

1 tsp. flaky sea salt

4 beets (2 lbs.), peeled and cut into wedges

2 medium red onions, cut into wedges

3 Tbsp. extra-virgin olive oil

2 Tbsp. fresh lemon juice

2 tsp. honey

¾ cup crumbled feta cheese

2 Tbsp. plain Greek yogurt

½ tsp. grated lemon zest

Pepper

2 heads of Little Gem or baby romaine lettuce (10 oz.)

Chopped cilantro and mint, for garnish

1. Preheat the oven to 375°. In a small skillet, toast the cumin seeds over low heat until fragrant, 2 minutes; let cool.

2. In a mortar, coarsely grind the cumin seeds with the salt. Transfer to a bowl and add the beets, onions and olive oil; toss to coat. Scrape the vegetables onto a rimmed baking sheet and roast for about 1 hour, stirring occasionally, until tender. Let cool to room temperature.

3. In a bowl, whisk the lemon juice and honey. In another bowl, mix the feta, yogurt and lemon zest so it remains a bit chunky. Season with pepper.

4. Arrange lettuce on plates. Top with beets and onions; drizzle with lemon honey. Top with feta dressing; season with pepper. Garnish with cilantro and mint. —*Tara Stevens*

GRILLED TOMATO CROSTINI

Total 30 min; Serves 4

4 tomatoes (1 lb.), quartered

1 pint grape or cherry tomatoes (10 oz.)

1 pint small mixed heirloom tomatoes, halved if large

½ cup extra-virgin olive oil, plus more for drizzling

Kosher salt and pepper

Four ¾-inch-thick slices of ciabatta

1 garlic clove, halved

20 small basil leaves

1. Light a grill. Arrange four 12-by-24-inch sheets of heavy-duty foil on a work surface. Mound the tomatoes in the center of each sheet, drizzle with the ½ cup of olive oil and season with salt and pepper. Fold up the foil to create tight packets. Poke small holes in the top of each packet.

2. Set the packets on the grill and cover. Grill over moderately high heat for about 18 minutes, until the tomatoes begin to soften and burst. Grill the ciabatta until toasted and charred in spots, about 1 minute per side. Transfer to plates and rub with the garlic halves.

Suggested Pairing

Serve a sparkling wine such as Cava with the frittata. Pair crostini with a crisp rosé.

Cheese Enchiladas
+ Skillet Corn and Peppers
+ Crudités à la Mexicaine

For a quick meal at home, chef Aarón Sánchez reaches for canned red chile sauce, such as one from Las Palmas. "It's old-school, very straightforward," he says. Sánchez sometimes adds shredded braised chicken to his enchiladas for a heartier meal. Punch up the menu with a raw vegetable platter from chef David Tanis and Linton Hopkins' spicy skillet corn topped with cilantro-lime mayonnaise. Add margaritas? Yes, please.

CHEESE ENCHILADAS WITH RED CHILE SAUCE

Active 10 min; Total 35 min; Serves 4

2 cups store-bought red chile sauce

½ cup vegetable oil

12 corn tortillas

12 oz. mozzarella, shredded (3 cups)

4 scallions including green tops, chopped (about 1 cup)

1. Preheat the oven to 350°. Spread ¼ cup of the red chile sauce in a 9-by-13-inch glass baking dish. In a medium skillet, heat the oil. Add the tortillas 1 at a time and fry over moderate heat just until pliable, about 5 seconds each. Transfer to a paper towel–lined baking sheet and blot the oil.

2. In a medium bowl, toss 2 cups of the shredded cheese with the scallions and ¾ cup of the red chile sauce. Arrange the tortillas on a work surface and spoon equal portions of the cheese mixture in the center of each one. Roll the tortillas into tight cylinders and transfer them to the prepared baking dish, seam side down. Spread the remaining 1 cup of red chile sauce over the enchiladas and sprinkle with the remaining 1 cup of cheese. Bake the enchiladas until heated through and bubbling, about 20 minutes. Let cool for 5 minutes and serve. —*Aarón Sánchez*

How to Assemble Enchiladas

Gooey, saucy, cheesy enchiladas are a dinner favorite and very easy to make.

3. Place the tortilla seam side down in the prepared baking dish. Fill and roll the remaining tortillas.

1. Fry the tortillas one at a time in a shallow pan of oil until pliable, then blot on paper towels.

2. Spoon some of the cheese mixture into a tortilla and roll into a tight cylinder.

4. Top the filled enchiladas with sauce and cheese according to the recipe directions.

SKILLET CORN AND PEPPERS WITH CILANTRO-LIME MAYO

Total 45 min; Serves 4

2 ears of corn, shucked, kernels cut off (2 cups) and cobs reserved

½ cup mayonnaise

½ cup packed cilantro leaves

½ tsp. finely grated lime zest, plus 1 Tbsp. fresh lime juice

Kosher salt and pepper

2 Tbsp. vegetable oil

12 Padrón peppers or 4 jalapeños, halved

1 Tbsp. unsalted butter

1. In a medium saucepan, simmer the corn cobs in 1 cup of water until the broth has reduced to ¼ cup, about 10 minutes. Strain the broth; discard the cobs.

2. Meanwhile, in a blender, combine the mayonnaise with the cilantro, lime zest and lime juice and puree until smooth. Season with salt.

3. In a cast-iron skillet, heat the oil until smoking. Add the corn kernels and peppers and season with salt. Cover and cook over moderately high heat until the corn starts to pop, 2 to 3 minutes. Stir the corn, cover and cook until the corn is lightly charred, about 2 minutes longer. Add the corn broth and simmer until nearly evaporated, then stir in the butter. Season with salt and pepper.

4. Transfer the corn and peppers to a bowl, drizzle with some of the cilantro-lime mayonnaise and serve.
—*Linton Hopkins*

CRUDITÉS À LA MEXICAINE

Total 25 min; Serves 4 to 6

3 small Kirby or Japanese cucumbers, quartered lengthwise

2 medium carrots, halved crosswise and sliced into ¼-inch sticks

1 small bunch of radishes, halved or quartered if large

1 Tbsp. kosher salt

1 tsp. pure chile powder, such as guajillo or Colorado

Key limes, halved

Arrange the vegetables on a platter. In a small bowl, combine the salt with the chile powder. Dip a lime half in the chile salt and dab the vegetables with it; squeeze the juice over the vegetables. Serve the crudités with the remaining lime halves and the remaining chile salt in a small bowl for dipping.
—*David Tanis*

+BONUS RECIPE: COCKTAIL
MARGARITA

Total 5 min; Makes 1 drink

2 oz. Reposado tequila

1 oz. fresh lime juice

1 oz. agave nectar

In a cocktail shaker, combine the tequila, lime juice and agave nectar . Fill the shaker with ice and shake well. Strain into a chilled, ice-filled double rocks glass. —*Julio Bermejo*

Grilled Tuna
+ Sweet-and-Sour Green Beans
+ Quinoa Pilaf

Chef Nick Fauchald uses smoked almonds and a touch of pimentón de la Vera (powdered, smoked Spanish red peppers) to add fabulous smoky flavors to the romesco sauce for the tuna. Balance those smoky flavors with tangy green beans and a sweet and savory quinoa pilaf. The romesco and pilaf can be made ahead of time and served at room temperature.

GRILLED TUNA WITH SMOKED-ALMOND ROMESCO SAUCE
Total 30 min; Serves 4

¼ cup plus 2 Tbsp. smoked almonds (2½ oz.)

One 3-inch piece of baguette, cubed

1 garlic clove

1 cup canned diced tomatoes

2 roasted red bell peppers from a jar, drained

2 Tbsp. sherry vinegar

¼ tsp. pimentón de la Vera

½ cup extra-virgin olive oil

Kosher salt and pepper

Four 1-inch-thick tuna steaks

1. Light a grill and oil the grate. In a food processor, coarsely chop the almonds, bread cubes and garlic. Add the tomatoes, roasted red peppers, sherry vinegar and pimentón and puree until smooth. With the machine on, gradually add the oil. Season the romesco sauce with salt and pepper.

2. Season the tuna with salt and pepper and grill over moderate heat, turning once, for 6 minutes for medium-rare, or 8 minutes for medium. Transfer the tuna to plates. Spoon some of the romesco sauce over the fish and pass the rest at the table. —*Nick Fauchald*

MAKE AHEAD The romesco sauce can be refrigerated for up to 1 week. Bring to room temperature before serving.

3 Easy Toppings for Grilled Tuna

Each of the recipes below makes enough sauce for four grilled tuna steaks.

LEMON-ANCHOVY BUTTER In a small bowl, combine 4 Tbsp. room-temperature butter with 1 Tbsp. chopped parsley, 1 tsp. fresh lemon juice, ½ tsp. anchovy paste and a pinch each of salt and pepper. Spread on grilled tuna steaks.

LEMON-CAPER SAUCE In a small glass or stainless-steel bowl, mash 3 Tbsp. drained capers with a fork. Stir in 6 Tbsp. extra-virgin olive oil, 1½ Tbsp. fresh lemon juice, ¼ cup chopped parsley, ½ tsp. salt and ¼ tsp. pepper. Drizzle on grilled tuna.

HERBED CREAM On a work surface, using a fork, mash 1 smashed garlic clove with ¼ tsp. salt. In a small bowl, blend the mashed garlic with ¼ cup each of mayonnaise, chopped basil and minced chives, ¼ tsp. black pepper and a pinch of cayenne. In a medium bowl, beat ⅓ cup heavy cream until stiff, then fold in the herbed mayonnaise. Top each grilled tuna steak with a tomato slice. Pass the herbed cream at the table.

QUINOA PILAF WITH DATES, OLIVES AND ARUGULA

Total 30 min; Serves 4

1½ cups white quinoa (9 oz.), rinsed and drained

⅓ cup chopped pitted Medjool dates

⅓ cup chopped pitted green olives

1 cup baby arugula

2 Tbsp. extra-virgin olive oil

2 Tbsp. fresh lemon juice

¼ cup sliced scallions

Kosher salt and pepper

1. In a medium saucepan of boiling water, cook the quinoa until tender, about 10 minutes. Drain and return to the pan. Cover and let stand for 10 minutes; fluff with a fork.

2. In a medium bowl, toss the quinoa with the dates, olives, arugula, olive oil, lemon juice and scallions. Season with salt and pepper. Serve chilled or at room temperature. —*Kay Chun*

SWEET-AND-SOUR GREEN BEANS

Total 15 min; Serves 4

¾ lb. green beans

2 Tbsp. extra-virgin olive oil

1 medium shallot, minced

2 Tbsp. cider vinegar

1 tsp. sugar

Kosher salt and pepper

1. In a steamer basket set over a large saucepan of boiling water, steam the green beans until bright green and crisp-tender, about 5 minutes.

2. In a medium skillet, heat the oil. Add the shallot and cook over high heat, stirring, until softened, about 2 minutes. Add the vinegar and sugar; stir to dissolve the sugar. Remove from the heat and add the beans. Season with salt and pepper, toss well and serve. —*Grace Parisi*

Suggested Pairing

Serve the grilled tuna with a light rosé from the Napa Valley.

Tequila-Chipotle Shrimp
+ Spanish Rice
+ Broccolini and Escarole Salad

Chef Deborah Schneider calls this easy 12-minute main dish "firing-squad shrimp" because it gets a little spice from a chipotle in adobo sauce. Pair the fiery shrimp with a smoky, charred Broccolini and escarole salad, then tame the heat with chef Lorena Herrera's tomato-packed Spanish rice.

TEQUILA-CHIPOTLE SHRIMP
Total 12 min; Serves 4

2 Tbsp. canola oil

½ cup finely chopped red onion

1 chipotle chile in adobo sauce, minced

One 15-oz. can diced tomatoes

Salt

Pepper

1 lb. large shrimp, shelled and deveined

¼ cup finely diced fresh pineapple

1 Tbsp. tequila

Chopped cilantro, for garnish

In a large skillet, heat the oil. Add the onion and chipotle and cook over moderately high heat, stirring, until just starting to soften, 2 to 3 minutes. Add the tomatoes and bring to a simmer. Season with salt and pepper, then nestle the shrimp in the sauce and cook, turning once, until just white throughout, about 5 minutes. Stir in the pineapple and tequila; garnish with cilantro and serve right away. —*Deborah Schneider*

Shrimp Sizing Demystified

At the seafood counter, you may see shrimp sold by size, such as medium, large and jumbo. However, these are unregulated terms that can differ across markets. A more precise measure is a number label that tells you how many of a particular size shrimp make up a pound. For example, a label of 31/35 means there are between 31 and 35 in a pound. If there's a letter U on the label, as in U-12, that means fewer than 12 yield a pound. The list on the right is a general guide for buying shrimp for both types of measurement.

1. Extra Jumbo; 16/20

2. Jumbo; 21/15

3. Extra Large; 26/30

4. Large; 31/35

5. Medium Large; 36/40

6. Medium; 41/50

7. Small; 51/60

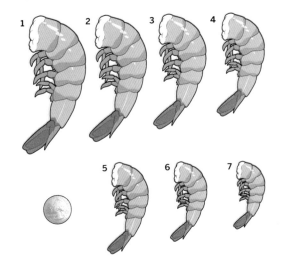

SPANISH RICE

Active 15 min; Total 50 min; Serves 8

2 medium tomatoes, chopped

1 medium onion, coarsely chopped

2 garlic cloves

Kosher salt and pepper

⅓ cup grapeseed oil

2 cups long-grain white rice

1 cup chicken stock or low-sodium broth

1. In a blender or food processor, puree the tomatoes with the onion, garlic and 1 teaspoon of salt until smooth.

2. In a large saucepan, heat the oil. Add the rice and cook over moderate heat, stirring, until lightly toasted, about 5 minutes. Pour in the tomato mixture and stock and bring to a boil. Cover and cook over low heat until the liquid has evaporated and the rice is tender, about 20 minutes. Remove the pan from the heat and let stand, covered, for 15 minutes. Fluff with a fork, season with salt and pepper and serve. —*Lorena Herrera*

MAKE AHEAD The cooked rice can stand, covered, for up to 30 minutes.

CHARRED BROCCOLINI AND ESCAROLE SALAD

Total 40 min; Serves 4

2 lbs. Broccolini, thick stems halved lengthwise

¼ cup extra-virgin olive oil, plus more for brushing

Kosher salt and pepper

Two ¾-inch-thick slices cut from a sourdough boule

1 garlic clove, halved

¼ cup Champagne vinegar

½ cup thinly sliced red onion

8 cups torn white and light green escarole leaves

1 fresh hot red chile—stemmed, seeded and very thinly sliced

1. Light a grill or preheat a grill pan. In a large bowl, toss the Broccolini with 2 tablespoons of the olive oil; season with salt and pepper. Grill over moderately high heat until lightly charred and crisp-tender, about 5 minutes. Transfer to a work surface; cut in half crosswise.

2. Brush the bread with olive oil and season with salt and pepper. Grill over moderately high heat, turning once, until lightly browned and crisp, about 3 minutes total. Transfer to a plate and rub with the cut sides of the garlic clove. Let cool slightly, then tear into bite-sized pieces.

3. In a serving bowl, mix the vinegar, onion and the remaining 2 tablespoons of olive oil. Add the escarole, Broccolini, garlic bread and chile and toss well. Season with salt and pepper, toss again and serve. —*Justin Chapple*

Suggested Pairing

Serve the shrimp with a fruit-forward, full-bodied California Chardonnay.

Fish Tacos
+ Spicy Pea Guacamole
+ Black Bean and Rice Salad

For her light and satisfying tacos, chef Deborah Schneider fills warm corn tortillas with meaty charred halibut and a brilliant, tart tomatillo salsa. Serve the fish tacos with a tangy black bean and yellow rice salad and chef Enrique Olvera's guacamole featuring creamy avocados and the lovely sweetness of green peas.

FISH TACOS WITH TOMATILLO-JALAPEÑO SALSA

Total 45 min; Serves 4

SALSA

4 medium tomatillos, husked, rinsed and quartered

½ cup lightly packed cilantro

2 small jalapeños, chopped

1½ Tbsp. fresh lime juice

1 tsp. vegetable oil

Kosher salt

TACOS

2 Tbsp. fresh lemon juice

1 Tbsp. extra-virgin olive oil

1 Tbsp. minced cilantro

1 small garlic clove, minced

1 lb. skinless halibut fillet, about ¾ inch thick

Kosher salt

Warm corn tortillas, chopped avocado and sliced red onion and cucumber, for serving

1. Make the salsa In a blender, combine all of the ingredients except the salt and puree until nearly smooth. Season with salt and transfer to a small bowl.

2. Make the tacos Heat a grill pan. In a large baking dish, whisk the lemon juice with the olive oil, cilantro and garlic. Add the fish and turn to coat. Season the fish all over with salt and grill over moderately high heat, turning once, until white throughout, 6 to 8 minutes. Transfer the fish to a platter and flake into large pieces with a fork. Serve in warm corn tortillas with the salsa, avocado, red onion and cucumber. —*Deborah Schneider*

MAKE AHEAD The salsa can be refrigerated for 3 days.

4 Chef Upgrades for Fish Tacos

ASIAN-STYLE
Tomas Lee, the chef at Hankook Taqueria in Atlanta, fries tilapia strips in a crisp panko crust for his tacos, which he tops with shredded green cabbage, lettuce, cilantro and sliced scallions. He serves them with a sauce of hoisin, mayonnaise, sweet pickle relish and lemon juice.

QUICKLY MARINATED
Cookbook author Phoebe Lapine adds flavor to thin white fish fillets by marinating them in a mix of lime juice, olive oil, honey, garlic, shallots and hot sauce before roasting.

DRY-RUBBED SALMON
For a heftier fish taco, Jeff Smith of Hourglass winery in Napa, California, rubs salmon fillets with cumin, chili powder, brown sugar and finely ground coffee before grilling. He tops the tacos with a cabbage slaw dressed with a spicy tomatillo-avocado sauce.

GRILLED SHRIMP
Tim Byres, the chef at Smoke in Dallas, grills shrimp on skewers, then tops the shrimp tacos with crunchy celery.

SPICY PEA GUACAMOLE

Total 20 min; Serves 4

1 serrano chile, chopped

½ cup chopped cilantro

½ cup thawed frozen peas

2 medium Hass avocados, peeled, pitted and chopped

Kosher salt

Tortilla chips, for serving

In a mortar, mash the chile with the cilantro. Add the peas and avocados and mash until well blended but still chunky. Season with salt and serve with chips. —*Enrique Olvera*

Suggested Pairing

Spritzy, lime-scented Vinno Verde from Portugal is fantastic with the spicy, cilantro-laced tacos.

BLACK BEAN AND YELLOW RICE SALAD

Total 45 min; Serves 4

3 Tbsp. vegetable oil

1 onion, chopped

2 garlic cloves, minced

¼ tsp. ground turmeric

½ tsp. ground cumin

Kosher salt and pepper

1½ cups long-grain rice

1 bay leaf

1⅔ cups canned black beans, drained and rinsed (from one 15-oz. can)

1 green bell pepper, chopped

2 tomatoes, diced

1 Tbsp. white wine vinegar

¼ cup chopped parsley

1 lime, quartered, for serving (optional)

1. In a medium saucepan, heat 2 tablespoons of the oil. Add the onion and cook over moderately low heat, stirring occasionally, until translucent, about 5 minutes. Stir in the garlic, turmeric, cumin, 1 teaspoon of salt, ¼ teaspoon of pepper and the rice. Cook, stirring frequently, for 2 minutes.

2. Add 2¾ cups of water and the bay leaf to the rice; bring to a simmer. Reduce the heat to low and cook, covered, until all of the liquid is absorbed and the rice is done, about 20 minutes. Remove the bay leaf.

3. In a large glass or stainless steel bowl, combine the rice, beans, bell pepper and tomatoes. Add the remaining 1 tablespoon of oil, ¼ teaspoon of salt, the vinegar and the parsley. Toss gently to combine. Serve with lime wedges, if using.

NOTE This festive bean-and-rice salad lends itself to endless variations. Replace the tomatoes with diced avocado; switch the bell pepper from green to red or yellow; stir in chopped scallions, red onion, or cilantro.

Seared Scallops
+ Cauliflower Puree
+ Spring Vegetable Panzanella

Chef Hugh Acheson, a F&W Best New Chef in 2002, flavors shallots with butter and Pinot Gris to create a sauce for scallops: "Pinot Gris loves shellfish," he says. Serve the saucy scallops with a springtime version of panzanella from chef Jeremy Fox featuring sunflower seed bread tossed with asparagus, peas, cucumbers and sunflower sprouts. A cauliflower puree completes the trio and can be made ahead, refrigerated and reheated.

SEARED SCALLOPS WITH PINOT GRIS BUTTER SAUCE
Active 25 min; Total 40 min; Serves 4

2 Tbsp. pine nuts

4 tsp. extra-virgin olive oil

2 medium shallots, minced

2 cups Pinot Gris

2 thyme sprigs

1 cup fish stock

1 Tbsp. heavy cream

1 stick unsalted butter, cut into ½-inch pieces and chilled

1 Tbsp. minced chives

Kosher salt and pepper

1 packed cup baby spinach

1 tsp. fresh lemon juice

2 Tbsp. vegetable oil

16 large sea scallops

½ tsp. Aleppo pepper flakes (optional)

1. In a skillet, toast the pine nuts over moderate heat until golden, 2 minutes; transfer to a plate and let cool. Lightly crush the nuts.

2. In a medium saucepan, heat 1 teaspoon of the olive oil. Add shallots; cook over moderate heat, stirring, until browned, 4 minutes. Add the wine and thyme; boil until reduced to ¼ cup, 15 minutes. Add stock and boil until reduced to ¼ cup, 9 minutes longer. Add the cream, bring to a boil and remove from the heat.

3. Strain the wine sauce into a clean saucepan. Whisk in the butter, 4 pieces at a time, until the sauce is thickened and smooth; set the pan over low heat as necessary to help melt the butter. Stir in the chives and season with salt and pepper. Remove from the heat.

4. In a medium bowl, toss the spinach with the lemon juice and the remaining tablespoon of olive oil; season with salt and pepper.

5. In the skillet, heat the vegetable oil. Season the scallops with salt and pepper, add to the skillet and cook over high heat, turning once, until browned but barely cooked through, 2 minutes per side. Transfer the scallops and spinach to plates. Garnish with the pine nuts and, if using, pepper flakes. Gently reheat the sauce, spoon on top and serve. —*Hugh Acheson*

Sea Scallops vs. Bay Scallops

SEA SCALLOPS
are meaty and big—up to two inches in diameter. They're best seared in a pan to develop a caramelized crust while keeping the interior tender and juicy.

BAY SCALLOPS
are much smaller than sea scallops. They have a short season, from fall to early winter. Prized for their sweeter meat, bay scallops are best cooked quickly to prevent them from becoming tough.

SPRING VEGETABLE AND SUNFLOWER PANZANELLA
Total 45 min; Serves 4 to 6

½ lb. sunflower seed bread or other seeded bread, cut into ½-inch cubes

1½ cups shelled English peas (from 1½ lbs. pods)

½ cup extra-virgin olive oil

¼ cup red wine vinegar

2 Tbsp. chopped dill

2 tsp. minced shallot

Kosher salt and pepper

4 Persian cucumbers (12 oz.), thinly sliced (3 cups)

½ lb. pencil-thin asparagus, cut into ½-inch pieces (1½ cups)

1 cup sunflower sprouts

2 Tbsp. sunflower seeds

Lebneh, for serving

1. Preheat the oven to 375°. Spread the bread on a baking sheet and bake for about 10 minutes, until golden and crisp. Let the croutons cool.

2. Meanwhile, in a small pot of salted boiling water, blanch the peas until tender, 2 minutes. Drain, then transfer to a bowl of ice water to stop the cooking. Drain well and pat dry.

3. In a large bowl, whisk the olive oil, vinegar, dill and shallot and season with salt and pepper; reserve half of the dressing in a small bowl. Add the cucumbers, asparagus, peas and croutons to the large bowl and toss to coat. Mound the salad on plates and top with the sunflower sprouts and seeds. Dollop a spoonful of lebneh on each salad and serve the remaining dressing on the side.
—*Jeremy Fox*

MAKE AHEAD The blanched English peas can be refrigerated overnight.

CAULIFLOWER PUREE WITH HORSERADISH AND CARAWAY
Total 20 min; Serves 4

1¾ lbs. cauliflower, cored and cut into florets

6 Tbsp. butter, plus more for serving

3 Tbsp. prepared horseradish, drained

Salt and pepper

Caraway seeds, for garnish

Set a steamer basket in a large saucepan filled with 1 inch of water. Add the cauliflower, cover and steam over high heat until tender, about 10 minutes. Transfer to a food processor and puree with the 6 tablespoons of butter and the horseradish. Season with salt and pepper. Transfer the puree to a serving bowl, garnish with caraway seeds and serve with butter. —*Justin Chapple*

MAKE AHEAD The cauliflower puree can be refrigerated for up to 2 days. Reheat gently before serving.

Suggested Pairing

Look for a dry, lightly-fruited Pinot Gris from Oregon or California to pair with the scallops.

Crab Cakes
+ Green Beans
+ Warm Potato Salad

"This is the best crab cake recipe you will ever find," claims chef and food writer Andrew Zimmern. "If you don't overmix, and don't pack your mounds too tightly, you will experience pure, unadulterated crab cake heaven." On your journey to crab cake heaven, don't miss the green beans in mustard-seed butter and warm potato salad.

Know Your Types of Crabmeat

COLOSSAL AND JUMBO LUMP Colossal is the largest, whole unbroken pieces of crabmeat. It's derived from the pair of muscles connected to the crab's swimming legs. Jumbo is the corresponding meat from smaller crabs. Both are luxurious in texture and best in preparations where whole pieces are prized, like crab cocktails and crab cakes.

BACKFIN These flakes of white meat are comprised of broken pieces of jumbo lump and the special grade. Try it in dips, salads, casseroles or in a seafood stuffing.

SPECIAL A less expensive alternative to backfin, these shreds and flakes of crabmeat come from the body of the crab. The special grade is often used in bisques and chowders.

SUPER LUMP A combination of broken jumbo lump and body meat from the shell, super lump is perfect in pastas and risotto.

BALTIMORE-STYLE CRAB CAKES

Active 25 min; Total 1 hr 25 min; Serves 4

½ cup mayonnaise

1 large egg, beaten

1 Tbsp. Dijon mustard

1 Tbsp. Worcestershire sauce

½ tsp. hot sauce

1 lb. jumbo lump crabmeat, picked over

20 saltine crackers, finely crushed

¼ cup canola oil

Lemon wedges, for serving

1. In a small bowl, whisk the mayonnaise with the egg, mustard, Worcestershire sauce and hot sauce until smooth.

2. In a medium bowl, lightly toss the crabmeat with the cracker crumbs. Gently fold in the mayonnaise mixture. Cover and refrigerate for at least 1 hour.

3. Scoop the crab mixture into eight ⅓-cup mounds, then lightly pack into 8 patties, about 1½ inches thick. In a large skillet, heat the oil until shimmering. Add crab cakes; cook over moderately high heat until deeply golden and heated through, about 3 minutes per side. Transfer the crab cakes to plates and serve with lemon wedges.
—Andrew Zimmern

MAKE AHEAD The crab cakes can be prepared through Step 2 and refrigerated overnight.

GREEN BEANS WITH MUSTARD-SEED BUTTER

Total 30 min; Serves 4

1 Tbsp. yellow mustard seeds

2 medium shallots, thinly sliced

⅓ cup sherry vinegar

¼ cup heavy cream

½ stick unsalted butter, softened

2 Tbsp. whole-grain mustard

Kosher salt and freshly ground pepper

2 lbs. green beans, trimmed

1. In a large skillet, toast mustard seeds over moderately high heat, shaking pan frequently, until they pop and start to brown, about 30 seconds. Transfer to a plate and let cool.

2. Add the shallots, vinegar and 2 tablespoons of water to the skillet and simmer over moderately low heat until the liquid is reduced to 1½ teaspoons, about 7 minutes. Add the cream and simmer over moderate heat until thickened, about 3 minutes. Transfer to a bowl and let cool to room temperature, then stir in the butter, mustard and toasted mustard seeds. Season with salt and pepper.

3. In a large pot of boiling salted water, cook the green beans until crisp-tender, about 4 minutes. Drain the beans, pat dry and transfer to a large bowl. Add the mustard-seed butter, season with salt and pepper, toss and serve.

MAKE AHEAD The mustard-seed butter can be refrigerated for up to 3 days or frozen for up to 1 month. Let the butter return to room temperature before using. The cooked green beans can be refrigerated overnight; blanch in boiling water or steam until heated through. —*Marcia Kiesel*

WARM POTATO SALAD WITH ARUGULA

Active 10 min; Total 40 min; Serves 4

1½ lbs. white potatoes, scrubbed and cut into ½-inch wedges

3½ Tbsp. extra-virgin olive oil

Kosher salt and freshly ground pepper

1 Tbsp. grainy mustard

2¼ tsp. sherry vinegar

½ small sweet onion, thinly sliced (1 cup)

2½ oz. baby arugula (4 cups)

1. Preheat the oven to 425°. Scatter the potato wedges on a large rimmed baking sheet, drizzle with 1½ tablespoons olive oil and toss until coated. Season with salt and pepper; roast until browned and crisp, about 25 minutes.

2. In a small bowl, whisk the remaining 2 tablespoons of olive oil with the mustard and vinegar and season with salt and pepper. In a large bowl, toss the potatoes with the onion and arugula. Top with the dressing, toss again and serve right away. —*Paul Vivant*

+BONUS RECIPE: COCKTAIL
GIN AND TONIC

Total 5 min; Makes 1 drink

Ice

1½ oz. gin, preferably Plymouth

4 oz. chilled tonic water, preferably Schweppes

1 or 2 lime wedges, for garnish

Fill a chilled highball glass with ice. Add the gin and tonic water and stir well. Garnish with lime wedge.
—*Todd Thrasher*

Salmon Papillotes
+ Pasta with Asparagus Pesto
+ Buttermilk-Dressed Spring Greens

Cooking the salmon en papillote makes for a quick and easy dinner with almost no cleanup. Also, cooking in parchment paper preserves the tenderness of the salmon and the crisp-tender texture of the Broccolini. Carry out the springtime theme by making an asparagus pesto to toss with pasta and serving an elegant spring greens salad from chef Eli Dahlin.

SALMON, BROCCOLINI AND FRESH RED CHILE PAPILLOTES
Active 15 min; Total 30 min; Serves 4

1 lb. Broccolini

Four 6-oz. skinless center-cut salmon fillets

8 thin slices of lemon

1 Fresno chile, thinly sliced into rings

6 Tbsp. extra-virgin olive oil

Kosher salt and pepper

1. Preheat the oven to 425°. Lay 4 large sheets of parchment paper on a work surface. Divide the Broccolini among the sheets and top each mound with a salmon fillet, 2 lemon slices and chile rings; drizzle each fillet with 1½ tablespoons of olive oil and season with salt and pepper. Fold the parchment over the fish, then fold the edge over itself in small pleats to seal the papillotes.

2. Transfer the papillotes to a large baking sheet and bake for 15 minutes, until slightly puffed. Carefully snip the packets open with scissors and serve. —*Justin Chapple*

Know Your Salmon

KING (OR CHINOOK) SALMON The largest and often the most expensive of the species, king salmon yields thick, meaty fillets with a buttery, silky texture. The color of the flesh can range from ivory to deep red, depending on the fish's diet. King salmon is wonderful grilled or seared—it will develop a crisp skin and crust while the interior stays medium-rare.

SOCKEYE (OR RED) SALMON The darkest of the salmons, sockeye has vivid red flesh and full flavor. It's leaner than the king salmon, so it's best served raw or cooked at low temperatures (for example, slow roasted or poached in oil) to keep it from drying out.

COHO (OR SILVER SALMON) Coho is milder and lighter in color than king salmon. Coho can be cooked similarly to king salmon but at a lower temperature since it's less fatty. Coho also takes well to curing, as in gravlax, or smoking.

CHUM (OR KETA OR DOGS) Salmon chum is smaller salmon. Mild in flavor, it is most often canned and rarely seen as fresh fillets at markets.

BUTTERMILK-DRESSED SPRING GREENS

Total 20 min; Serves 4

½ cup buttermilk

¼ cup cottage cheese (4% milk fat)

1 Tbsp. red wine vinegar

½ tsp. Dijon mustard

½ tsp. minced shallot

1½ Tbsp. finely chopped tarragon

Kosher salt and pepper

1 small head of red leaf lettuce, torn

1 head of Boston lettuce, torn

½ cup smoked almonds (2½ oz.), chopped, for garnish

1. In a blender, puree the buttermilk with the cottage cheese, vinegar, Dijon and shallot until smooth. Scape the dressing into a small bowl and stir in the tarragon; season with salt and pepper.

2. In a serving bowl, toss the lettuces with some of the dressing. Garnish with the almonds and serve, passing the remaining dressing at the table. —*Eli Dahlin*

PASTA WITH ASPARAGUS PESTO

Total 30 min; Serves 4

¾ lb. spaghetti

1 lb. asparagus, trimmed and coarsely chopped

½ cup extra-virgin olive oil, plus more for drizzling

¼ cup freshly grated Parmigiano-Reggiano cheese

½ cup basil leaves, torn if large

1 Tbsp. fresh lemon juice

Salt and pepper

1. In a large pot of salted boiling water, cook the pasta until al dente. Drain, reserving ¼ cup of the pasta cooking water.

2. Meanwhile, in a food processor, pulse the asparagus until finely chopped. Transfer to a large bowl. Stir in the ½ cup of olive oil along with the cheese, basil and lemon juice; season the pesto with salt and pepper. Add the hot pasta and reserved cooking water and toss until the pasta is well coated with pesto. Season with salt and pepper, drizzle with olive oil and serve. —*Kay Chun*

Suggested Pairing

Pair the salmon and pasta with a bright, cool-climate Chardonnay from California's Sonoma Coast.

Glazed Chicken Legs
+ Roasted Broccoli
+ Fried Rice

These chicken legs are great hot out of the oven, but leftovers make a killer chicken salad. For an easy weeknight dinner, serve the sweet and spicy chicken legs with a comforting vegetable-packed rice infused with ginger and a roasted broccoli side dish offering a kick of Sriracha.

SOY-MAPLE-GLAZED CHICKEN LEGS

Active 10 min; Total 1 hr 10 min; Serves 4

⅓ cup maple syrup

¼ cup soy sauce

1 Tbsp. rice wine vinegar

Kosher salt and pepper

2 lbs. chicken legs, split

1. Preheat the oven to 425°. In a medium bowl, stir together the syrup, soy sauce, vinegar, 1½ teaspoons of salt and ¾ teaspoon of pepper. Toss the chicken with the marinade and let stand for 20 minutes.

2. Place the chicken along with the marinade on an aluminum foil–lined baking sheet and roast until golden brown and cooked through, 40 to 45 minutes. Season with salt and pepper and serve. —Ian Knauer

SRIRACHA-ROASTED BROCCOLI

Total 30 min; Serves 4

3 Tbsp. extra-virgin olive oil

2 Tbsp. Sriracha

1 Tbsp. soy sauce

½ tsp. sesame oil

1 tsp. brown sugar

3 cloves garlic, crushed or minced

1¼ lbs. broccoli crowns, stems peeled and heads halved

Fresh cracked black pepper

¼ cup chopped cilantro

1. Preheat the oven to 425°. In a bowl, whisk together the olive oil, Sriracha, soy sauce, sesame oil, brown sugar and garlic.

2. Place the broccoli on a baking pan. Drizzle the oil mixture over the broccoli. Toss to coat evenly. Season with pepper, then spread the broccoli in an even layer.

3. Roast for 10 minutes, turn the broccoli, then continue roasting for 5 more minutes, or until tender and the edges are crisped.

4. Transfer the broccoli to a bowl, toss with the chopped cilantro and serve. —Todd Porter and Diane Cu

KALE-AND-SHIITAKE FRIED RICE

Total 40 min; Serves 4

¼ cup vegetable oil

One ½-inch piece of fresh ginger, peeled and minced

6 scallions, thinly sliced

Kosher salt

¾ lb. shiitake mushrooms, stems discarded, caps sliced

6 cups coarsely chopped curly kale leaves (about half of a medium bunch)

2 garlic cloves, minced

4 cups day-old cooked short-grain white rice

3 large eggs, lightly beaten

1½ Tbsp. rice wine vinegar

1 Tbsp. oyster sauce

1. In a wok or very large skillet, heat 3 tablespoons of the oil. Add the ginger, scallions and a pinch of salt. Cook over moderately high heat, stirring constantly, until the ginger and scallions are tender, about 2 minutes. Add the sliced shiitakes and a generous pinch of salt and cook, stirring frequently, until tender, about 5 minutes. Add the kale, season with salt and stir-fry until wilted, 2 to 3 minutes. Add the garlic and cook for 1 minute more. Add the cooked rice and stir-fry until heated through, about 3 minutes.

2. Make a well in the rice and add the remaining 1 tablespoon of oil. When the oil is shimmering, add the eggs. Cook without stirring until the eggs begin to set at the edge. Using a spatula, scramble the eggs until just set. Stir the eggs into the rice along with the vinegar and oyster sauce and season with salt. Serve immediately. —David Lebovitz

Suggested Pairing

Serve the glazed chicken legs with a fruity, full-bodied old vine Zinfandel from Sonoma.

Spring Beef Stew
+ Buttermilk-Parmesan Biscuits
+ Boston Lettuce Salad

In this lovely, lighter-than-most beef stew, F&W's Justin Chapple simmers chuck until it's super tender before adding carrots, peas, spinach and dill. Accompanying the beef stew are Parmesan biscuits from chef Shawn McClain who says that the key to making these biscuits light and flaky is working the dough as little as possible. The simple side salad comes from Katherine Anderson who uses radishes from her family's Oxbow Farm and tosses them with tender Boston lettuce leaves.

SPRING BEEF STEW
Active 30 min; Total 2 hr; Serves 4 to 6

2 Tbsp. extra-virgin olive oil

2 lbs. beef chuck, cut into 1½-inch pieces

Kosher salt and pepper

1 qt. chicken stock or low-sodium broth

6 shallots, halved

½ lb. carrots, cut into 2-inch lengths

1½ cups frozen peas

5 oz. curly spinach

2 Tbsp. chopped dill

Crusty bread, for serving

1. In a large saucepan, heat the olive oil until shimmering. Season the meat with salt and pepper and add it to the saucepan in a single layer. Cook over moderately high heat, turning occasionally, until browned all over, about 10 minutes. Add the stock and shallots and bring to a boil. Simmer over low heat until the meat is tender, about 1½ hours.

2. Add the carrots to the saucepan and simmer until tender, about 12 minutes. Add the peas, spinach and dill and cook until the spinach is wilted, about 2 minutes. Ladle the stew into bowls and serve with crusty bread. —*Justin Chapple*

MAKE AHEAD The stew can be refrigerated overnight. Reheat gently before serving.

Best Beef Cuts for Stew

CHUCK Chuck, an inexpensive cut from the neck, shoulder and upper arm, is tough but flavorful, with a good amount of connective tissue. It becomes nicely tender when stewed for at least 90 minutes.

BRISKET This huge cut from the breast is usually barbecued or braised. When cut into pieces, it works well in stews. After stewing for at least two hours, the chunks will pull into delicious shreds.

SHORT RIBS This cut gets its name not because the ribs are short in length, but because they're from the short plate of the cow. Highly marbled (and pricier than both chuck and brisket), short ribs turn fabulously succulent and tender when slow-simmered in stews.

BUTTERMILK-PARMESAN BISCUITS

Active 25 min; Total 45 min; Makes 2 dozen

4 cups all-purpose flour

1½ cups freshly grated Parmigiano-Reggiano cheese

2 Tbsp. finely chopped thyme

2 Tbsp. baking powder

1 Tbsp. kosher salt

1 tsp. sugar

½ tsp. baking soda

6 Tbsp. vegetable shortening, chilled

6 Tbsp. unsalted butter, cut into small pieces and chilled

1½ cups buttermilk, chilled

1. Preheat the oven to 425°. In a large bowl, whisk together the flour, Parmigiano-Reggiano, thyme, baking powder, salt, sugar and baking soda. Using a pastry cutter or 2 knives, cut in the chilled shortening and butter until the mixture resembles coarse meal. Add the buttermilk and mix gently until just incorporated.

2. On a floured work surface, using a rolling pin, gently roll out the dough to a 13-inch round, about ½ inch thick. With a 2½-inch fluted biscuit cutter, cut out as many biscuits as possible. Transfer to 2 large baking sheets, leaving about 1 inch between biscuits. Gather the dough scraps, gently press them together and cut out 5 or 6 more biscuits.

3. Bake the biscuits for about 18 minutes, until they are golden brown and risen. Serve hot or warm.

MAKE AHEAD The biscuits can be kept at room temperature for up to 3 hours; reheat before serving. —Shawn McClain

BOSTON LETTUCE AND RADISH SALAD

Total 25 min; Serves 4

2 Tbsp. extra-virgin olive oil

1 Tbsp. sherry vinegar

¼ tsp. Dijon mustard

Kosher salt and freshly ground black pepper

1 bunch of radishes (about 10), tops reserved for another use, radishes very thinly sliced

2 small heads of Boston lettuce, outer leaves discarded, tender inner leaves torn

In a large bowl, whisk the olive oil with the vinegar and mustard and season with salt and pepper. Add the radishes and lettuce, toss well and serve right away.

—Katherine Anderson

Suggested Pairing

Serve the beef stew with a peppery, fruit-dense California Syrah.

Spiced Brown Sugar Ham

+ Classic Potato Salad
+ Sautéed Spring Greens

Chef Kevin Gillespie says that the secret to this tender ham is keeping it wrapped in foil while it's cooking and resting, letting it reabsorb any moisture released during the cooking process. You'll have some leftovers for a meal later on in the week and that's a good thing. Serve the ham with a classic springtime favorite—potato salad—from Melissa Rubel Jacobson and sautéed spring greens accented with smoky bacon, hot chile and the pop of mustard seeds.

SPICED BROWN SUGAR HAM WITH APPLE JUS

Active 20 min; Total 5 hr 30 min; Serves 8 to 10

One 1-lb. box light brown sugar

2 Tbsp. freshly ground black pepper

1½ tsp. ground cloves

1½ tsp. ground cinnamon

One 8- to 10-lb. bone-in smoked ham, skin removed

3 medium Fuji apples—peeled, cored and thinly sliced

2 Tbsp. apple cider vinegar

Kosher salt

1. Preheat the oven to 350°. In a medium bowl, mix the sugar with the pepper, cloves and cinnamon.

2. Place the ham fat side up on two large pieces of aluminum foil and, using your hands, rub the sugar mixture all over the top and side; it should form a thick layer. Wrap the ham tightly in the foil and transfer to a large roasting pan. Bake for about 3 hours, until glossy on the outside and a thermometer inserted in the thickest part of the meat registers 125°. Transfer the ham to a work surface and let rest in the foil at room temperature until cool enough to handle, about 2 hours.

3. Unwrap the ham and slice the meat; transfer to a large platter and tent with foil to keep warm. Pour the accumulated juices into a large measuring cup and spoon off any fat. You should have about 3¼ cups.

4. In a medium saucepan, combine the sliced apples with 2 tablespoons of water. Cover and cook over moderate heat, stirring occasionally, until tender, about 10 minutes. Using a slotted spoon, transfer the apples to a blender and puree with the ham juices and vinegar until smooth. Strain the apple jus through a fine-mesh sieve set over a gravy boat and season with salt. Serve the ham, passing the apple jus at the table. —*Kevin Gillespie*

NOTE Refrigerate any leftover ham for up to 4 days.

How to Carve Bone-In Ham

1. On a cutting board, trim a few slices off the bottom of the ham, to form a flat base. Flip the ham to rest on this trimmed side.

2. Hold the ham in place with a carving fork. Starting at narrower shank end, slice the ham crosswise all the way to the bone.

Slice only as much as needed; leftover ham keeps better when on the bone.

3. Cut lengthwise along the bone and remove slices with a fork.

SAUTÉED SPRING GREENS WITH BACON AND MUSTARD SEEDS

Total: 20 min; Serves 4

2 oz. thick-cut bacon, finely diced

2 Tbsp. extra-virgin olive oil

1 large shallot, thinly sliced

1 hot red chile, seeded and finely chopped

1 Tbsp. yellow mustard seeds

1¼ lbs. mixed young spring greens, such as dandelion, mustard, collards, Tuscan kale and spinach, stems and inner ribs trimmed, leaves cut into ribbons

Salt and freshly ground pepper

1 Tbsp. white wine vinegar

In a large skillet, cook the diced bacon in the olive oil over moderate heat, stirring, until golden, about 3 minutes. Add the shallot, chile and mustard seeds and cook until softened, 2 to 3 minutes. Add the greens, season with salt and pepper and cook, tossing frequently, until wilted and tender, 5 to 6 minutes. Stir in the vinegar and serve. —*Grace Parisi*

NOTE If you want to omit the bacon, heat the oil in the skillet, cook the shallot, chile and mustard seeds until softened, then proceed with recipe as directed.

CLASSIC POTATO SALAD

Active 15 min; Total 40 min; Serves 4

1½ lbs. baby Yukon Gold or baby red potatoes (about 2 inches each), scrubbed

Kosher salt and pepper

¼ cup mayonnaise

1 Tbsp. distilled white vinegar

1 tsp. Dijon mustard

1 scallion, thinly sliced

1 Tbsp. chopped flat-leaf parsley

¼ celery rib, cut into ¼-inch dice

1. In a large saucepan, cover potatoes with cold water and season water with salt. Bring to a boil over high heat and cook the potatoes until tender, about 15 minutes. Drain and let stand until cool enough to handle, about 10 minutes.

2. Meanwhile, in a large bowl, whisk the mayonnaise with the vinegar and mustard and season with salt and pepper. Stir in the scallions, parsley and celery. Halve the potatoes crosswise and fold them into the dressing. Serve warm or at room temperature. —*Melissa Rubel Jacobson*

Suggested Pairing

Serve a Cabernet Sauvignon Rosé with refreshing acidity with the brown sugar ham.

Slow Cooker Corned Beef

+ Irish Brown Bread
+ Steamed Leeks

This classic Irish-American dish gets simplified in the slow cooker, giving you time to bake the bread and steam the leeks as well as sip on a Guinness. Even though this bread is dense and hearty, it requires no yeast and therefore no rising time. Chef Cathal Armstrong says he likes it best "fresh from the oven and with lots of Kerrygold butter."

SLOW COOKER CORNED BEEF WITH CABBAGE, CARROTS AND POTATOES

Active 15 min; Total 10 hr 15 min; Serves 6

One 6½-lb. corned beef

6 heads of garlic

6 medium carrots, peeled

6 medium red potatoes, halved

One 2-lb. head of green cabbage, cut into 6 wedges

Mustard and horseradish, for serving

1. Put the corned beef in a large slow cooker. Add the garlic and 6 cups of water, cover and cook on high for 5½ hours.

2. Add another 4 cups of water and cook on low until corned beef is tender, about 1½ hours. Transfer corned beef to a large pan and cover with foil. Discard garlic.

3. Add the carrots and potatoes to the cooker, cover and cook on high until almost tender, about 2 hours. Add the cabbage wedges and cook until tender, about 45 minutes.

4. On a carving board, cut the corned beef across the grain into ⅓-inch-thick slices. Keeping the slices together, return the meat to the slow cooker and cook on low until heated through, about 15 minutes. Serve the corned beef and vegetables in the cooking liquid, passing mustard and horseradish at the table. —*Marcia Kiesel*

MAKE AHEAD The corned beef and vegetables can be refrigerated in the cooking liquid overnight and reheated gently.

IRISH BROWN BREAD

Active 10 min; Total 1 hr; Makes 1 loaf

3 cups whole wheat flour

1 cup all-purpose flour

1 tsp. baking soda

1 tsp. salt

1¼ cups buttermilk

1 large egg, lightly beaten

1. Preheat the oven to 375°. Butter an 8-by-5-inch metal loaf pan. In a large bowl, whisk both flours with the baking soda and salt. In a small bowl, whisk the buttermilk with the egg; stir into the dry ingredients with a wooden spoon until a rough dough forms.

2. Transfer the dough to a lightly floured work surface and knead until smooth. Form the dough into a loaf and put it in the prepared pan. Bake for about 50 minutes, until the bread has risen about ½ inch above the rim of the pan. Once unmolded, the loaf should sound hollow when tapped on the bottom. Let cool to warm or room temperature, then slice and serve. —*Cathal Armstrong*

Suggested Pairing

Try a light-bodied, fruity red like a Beaujolais or Grenache or a stout like Guinness.

STEAMED LEEKS WITH MUSTARD-SHALLOT VINAIGRETTE

Total 35 min; Serves 4

2 large leeks, cut into 2-by-½-inch strips

1 small shallot, minced

1 Tbsp. Dijon mustard

1 Tbsp. red wine vinegar

1 tsp. balsamic vinegar

¼ cup extra-virgin olive oil

Kosher salt and pepper

1 Tbsp. chopped parsley

1. In a saucepan fitted with a steamer basket, bring 1 inch of water to a boil. Add the leeks, cover and steam until just tender, about 5 minutes. Drain the leeks, pat dry and refrigerate until chilled, about 10 minutes.

2. Meanwhile, in a small bowl, combine the shallot with the mustard and both vinegars. Whisk in the olive oil and season with salt and pepper.

3. Mound the steamed leeks on plates. Drizzle them with the vinaigrette, sprinkle with the parsley and serve.
—*Stéphanie Vivier*

MAKE AHEAD The steamed leeks and the mustard-shallot vinaigrette can be refrigerated separately overnight.

+BONUS RECIPE: COCKTAIL
LADY IRISH

Total 10 min; Makes 1 drink

Ice

⅔ oz. Irish whiskey, preferably Bushmills

⅔ oz. oloroso sherry

½ oz. Red Currant Syrup or grenadine

⅓ oz. fresh lemon juice

1 tsp. cane syrup

1⅔ oz. chilled Champagne

1 small bunch of red currants, for garnish (optional)

Fill a cocktail shaker with ice. Add all of the remaining ingredients except the Champagne and the garnish and shake well. Strain the drink into a large chilled coupe and top with the Champagne. Garnish with the red currants.
—*Sean Maldoon*

How to Clean Leeks

1. Trim off the leek's root and cut off the dark green part of the leek.

2. Halve the leek lengthwise and slice it according to the recipe directions.

3. Place the sliced leeks in a large bowl of cold water and swish around with your hands. The leeks will float to the top while any grit will sink to the bottom.

4. Lift the leeks from the surface of the water and drain them in a colander.

Roast Leg of Lamb
+ Peas with Spring Onions
+ Steamed New Potatoes

Chef Curtis Stone makes easy work of a leg of lamb, starting with it at room temperature, roasting it with fragrant rosemary and garlic and serving it with an easy pan sauce. When spring arrives, chef Mike Lata uses delicate peas and pea shoots to make a simple green side dish that's perfect with lamb. Complete the menu with another spring classic—Daniel Patterson's steamed new potatoes with dandelion greens.

ROAST LEG OF LAMB WITH ROSEMARY
Active 45 min; Total 2 hr 30 min; Serves 6 to 8

One 4½-lb. semi-boneless leg of lamb, at room temperature (shank end, hip bone removed)

Kosher salt and pepper

3 Tbsp. extra-virgin olive oil

2 Tbsp. finely grated lemon zest

4 garlic cloves, minced

20 large rosemary sprigs

½ cup red wine vinegar

2 Tbsp. turbinado sugar

1 cup lightly packed mint leaves

1. Preheat the oven to 350°. Season the lamb all over with salt and pepper. In a very large, deep skillet, heat 2 tablespoons of the olive oil until shimmering. Add the lamb and cook over moderately high heat, turning occasionally, until browned all over, about 12 minutes. Transfer to a plate.

2. In a small bowl, whisk the lemon zest with the garlic and remaining 1 tablespoon of olive oil. Rub the mixture all over the lamb.

3. Arrange 9 long pieces of kitchen string crosswise on a large rimmed baking sheet, 1 inch apart. Arrange 10 rosemary sprigs across the strings and set the lamb on top. Cover the lamb with the remaining rosemary, then pull up each piece of string and tie tightly to secure the rosemary and form a neat roast.

4. Roast the lamb on the baking sheet for about 1 hour and 20 minutes, until an instant-read thermometer inserted in the thickest part of the meat registers 130°. Transfer the lamb to a carving board and let rest for 30 minutes.

5. Meanwhile, in a small saucepan, bring the vinegar, sugar and ½ cup of water just to a simmer, stirring to dissolve the sugar. Remove from the heat, add the mint leaves and let stand for 30 minutes. Season the sauce with salt.

6. Untie the lamb and discard the rosemary sprigs. Carve the lamb and serve with the mint sauce. —Curtis Stone

How to Carve Bone-In Leg of Lamb

1. On a cutting board, place the lamb on its side with the shank bone facing away from you. Trim a few slices off the bottom, to form a flat base. Flip the lamb to rest on this trimmed side.

2. Hold the lamb in place with a carving fork. Cut thin, even slices (¼ inch to ½ inch thick) across the grain, holding the knife perpendicular to the cutting board. Slice only as much as needed; leftover lamb keeps better when left intact on the bone.

3. Cut lengthwise along the bone and remove the slices with a fork.

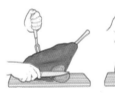

PEAS AND PEA SHOOTS WITH SPRING ONIONS AND MINT

Total 20 min; Serves 4

½ lb. frozen peas (2 cups)

1 Tbsp. extra-virgin olive oil

2 spring onions (bulbing), sliced ¼ inch thick (1½ cups)

Kosher salt and pepper

1½ Tbsp. unsalted butter

1½ cups lightly packed tender pea shoots or small watercress sprigs

¼ cup mint leaves

1. In a large saucepan of salted boiling water, cook the peas until just tender, about 3 minutes. Drain.

2. In the same saucepan, heat the olive oil. Add the onions and a pinch of salt, cover and cook over moderately low heat, stirring occasionally, until softened, 5 minutes. Stir in the peas, cover and cook until heated through, 1 minute. Stir in the butter, 1 tablespoon at a time. Remove from the heat and stir in the pea shoots until wilted. Stir in the mint, season with salt and pepper and serve. *—Mike Lata*

STEAMED NEW POTATOES WITH DANDELION GREENS SALSA VERDE

Active 20 min; Total 40 min; Serves 4

1 shallot, minced

2 Tbsp. Champagne or white wine vinegar

1 lb. small new potatoes

1 bunch dandelion greens (¾ lb.), trimmed

2 caperberries or 1 Tbsp. drained capers, minced

1 Tbsp. fresh lemon juice

½ cup fruity extra-virgin olive oil, plus more for drizzling

Sea salt and freshly ground black pepper

Sliced radishes, for garnish

1. In a medium bowl, combine the minced shallot and Champagne vinegar and let stand for 20 minutes.

2. Meanwhile, in a medium saucepan of boiling water, cook the potatoes until they are tender, about 15 minutes. Drain and slice the potatoes ⅓ inch thick.

3. Prepare a bowl of ice water. In a small pot of salted boiling water, cook the dandelion greens until they are tender, 7 to 8 minutes. Drain and transfer the greens to the ice bath to cool. Drain, squeezing out as much water as possible. Finely chop the greens and transfer them to the bowl with the vinegared shallot. Stir in the minced caperberries, lemon juice and ½ cup of olive oil. Season the dandelion salsa verde with sea salt and black pepper.

4. Spoon some of the dandelion salsa verde onto plates. Top with the warm potato slices and season with sea salt. Garnish with radishes, drizzle olive oil on top and serve.
—Daniel Patterson

Suggested Pairing

Serve this beautiful lamb with a bold red wine from Australia such as Shiraz or a French rosé with subtle berry and citrus notes.

summer

Avocado-and-Shrimp Salad
+ Zucchini-Feta Fritters
+ Tomato Soup

For this vibrant main dish shrimp salad, chef Jonathan Waxman makes his tangy goddess dressing red instead of the classic green, using roasted red bell peppers for color and flavor. The pretty, fresh-tasting tomato soup is chef David Chang's riff on Greek salad—it's topped with tomatoes, olives, honeyed cucumbers and feta. Accompany the salad and the soup with garden-fresh zucchini fritters made with herbs and feta. Chef Didem Şenol's fritters are terrific on their own or dipped into the yogurt-cucumber sauce.

AVOCADO-AND-SHRIMP SALAD
WITH RED GODDESS DRESSING
Total 30 min; Serves 4 to 6

1 roasted red bell pepper, chopped

1 shallot, minced

1 garlic clove, minced

1 tsp. minced jalapeño

3 Tbsp. plain yogurt

1 Tbsp. apple cider vinegar

1 tsp. fresh lemon juice

¼ cup plus 1 Tbsp. extra-virgin olive oil

Kosher salt

1 head of lettuce, torn into large pieces

¼ cup cilantro leaves

1 tsp. fresh lime juice

2 Hass avocados, cut into wedges

1 lb. cooked shrimp

1. In a blender, combine the roasted pepper, shallot, garlic, jalapeño, yogurt, vinegar and lemon juice and puree until smooth. Scrape the puree into a medium bowl and whisk in ¼ cup of the olive oil. Season with salt.

2. In a large bowl, toss the lettuce with the cilantro leaves, lime juice and the remaining 1 tablespoon of olive oil; season with salt. Arrange the dressed lettuce, avocado wedges and shrimp on plates and drizzle with some of the dressing. Serve the remaining Red Goddess dressing on the side.

—Jonathan Waxman

How to Pit an Avocado

1. Using a chef's knife, slice the avocado in half lengthwise, working around the pit.

2. Separate the two halves. Place the half containing the pit on a work surface. Firmly strike the pit with the knife.

3. Embed the blade in the pit and twist gently to remove it.

4. Using a large spoon, scoop out the avocado flesh from each half.

HERBED ZUCCHINI-FETA FRITTERS

Total 50 min; Serves 4 to 6

4 medium zucchini (about 1¾ lbs.), coarsely shredded

1 Tbsp. kosher salt plus more for seasoning

2 large eggs, lightly beaten

½ cup all-purpose flour

¼ cup chopped dill

¼ cup chopped parsley

¼ cup plus 2 Tbsp. chopped mint

½ cup crumbled feta cheese

½ tsp. freshly ground pepper, plus more for seasoning

1 medium cucumber, peeled, halved, seeded and coarsely chopped

1 cup Greek-style plain yogurt

Vegetable oil, for frying

1. Pile the shredded zucchini in a colander and sprinkle with 1 tablespoon of salt. Toss the zucchini well and let stand for 5 minutes. Squeeze out as much liquid as possible and transfer the zucchini to a large bowl. Stir in the eggs, flour, dill, parsley, ¼ cup of the mint and the feta. Stir in ½ teaspoon of pepper and refrigerate the fritter batter for about 10 minutes.

2. In a food processor, coarsely puree the chopped cucumber. Transfer to a medium bowl. Stir in the yogurt and the remaining 2 tablespoons of mint and season with salt and pepper.

3. Preheat the oven to 350°. In a medium saucepan, heat ½ inch of vegetable oil to 350°. Set a paper towel–covered baking sheet near the stove. Working in batches, drop rounded tablespoons of fritter batter into hot oil and fry, turning the fritters a few times, until browned and crisp, about 2 minutes. Using a slotted spoon, transfer fritters to the prepared baking sheet and repeat with remaining fritter batter. Discard the paper towels and reheat the fritters in the oven for about 3 minutes. Serve the zucchini fritters hot with the cucumber-yogurt sauce.
—*Didem Şenol*

MAKE AHEAD The cucumber-yogurt sauce can be refrigerated overnight. Serve the sauce lightly chilled.

TOMATO SOUP WITH FETA, OLIVES AND CUCUMBERS

Total 40 min; Serves 4

6 Tbsp. extra-virgin olive oil, plus more for drizzling

1 small red onion, thinly sliced

¾ cup pitted Niçoise olives

2 Tbsp. oregano leaves

3 Tbsp. red wine vinegar

1 Tbsp. sherry vinegar

Kosher salt

1 small Kirby cucumber, thinly sliced

1 Tbsp. honey

5 tomatoes, chopped

Freshly ground black pepper

4 oz. cherry tomatoes, halved

2 oz. feta cheese, preferably Greek, crumbled (½ cup)

Baby greens, for garnish

1. In a medium saucepan, heat the 6 tablespoons of oil. Add the onion, olives and oregano and cook over moderately low heat, stirring, until the onion is softened, about 7 minutes. Remove from the heat and stir in both vinegars. Season with salt. Cool to room temperature.

2. Meanwhile, in a bowl, toss the cucumber with ½ tablespoon of the honey and season with salt.

3. In a blender, puree the chopped tomatoes with the remaining ½ tablespoon of honey and season generously with salt and pepper.

4. Pour the soup into shallow bowls. Top with the onion-olive mixture, cherry tomatoes, cucumber slices and feta. Drizzle with olive oil, garnish with baby greens and serve.
—*David Chang*

Suggested Pairing

Serve a lively Provençal rosé with the shrimp salad.

Tuna Noodle Cazuela
+ Breadstick Twists
+ Golden Gazpacho

Jarred piquillo peppers and imported canned tuna from Spain add an Iberian twist to the classic American tuna casserole from Grace Parisi, making it more elegant but keeping it as simple and quick as the original. Serve with Susan Spungen's savory breadstick twists and a gazpacho made with yellow or orange cherry tomatoes and topped with avocado. The gazpacho can be made ahead and refrigerated overnight.

CREAMY TUNA NOODLE CAZUELA
Total 40 min; Serves 4

12 oz. farfalle pasta

4 Tbsp. unsalted butter

1 medium onion, finely chopped

2 Tbsp. all-purpose flour

3 cups whole milk or half-and-half

1½ cups frozen baby peas

¾ cup piquillo peppers, sliced (6 oz.)

½ cup freshly grated Parmigiano-Reggiano cheese

One 6-oz. can or jar solid white tuna in oil, drained and flaked

Salt and freshly ground pepper

½ cup panko (Japanese breadcrumbs)

1. Preheat the oven to 450°. Cook the farfalle pasta in a large pot of boiling salted water until al dente. Drain.

2. Meanwhile, in a large saucepan, melt 3 tablespoons of the butter. Add the onion and cook over high heat, stirring, until softened, about 3 minutes. Add the flour and cook, stirring, for 1 minute. Add the milk and bring to a boil. Cook the sauce over moderate heat, stirring occasionally, until thickened, about 3 minutes.

3. Add the farfalle pasta, frozen baby peas, sliced piquillo peppers, Parmigiano cheese and tuna and season with salt and pepper. Transfer the mixture to a large baking dish, a *cazuela* (casserole dish) or 4 individual gratin dishes.

4. In a small skillet, melt the remaining 1 tablespoon of butter. Add the panko and cook over moderate heat, stirring, until golden, about 1 minute. Sprinkle the panko over the casserole and bake for 10 minutes (5 minutes for individual gratins), or until bubbling. Serve right away.
—*Grace Parisi*

3 Uses for Canned Tuna

TONNATO SAUCE
Combine the tuna and the oil it's packed in (if it's in water, drain first) with lemon juice, capers, anchovy fillets, olive oil and a touch of mayo (or plain yogurt) in a blender and puree until smooth. Traditionally served on cold sliced veal (vitello tonnato), the sauce is great as a crudité dip, salad dressing on escarole or arugula, or drizzled on grilled chicken breasts. Use it as a sandwich spread for turkey sandwiches or as the base for potato salad.

TUNA-HUMMUS SALAD Replace the mayo in your favorite tuna salad recipe with hummus mixed with olive oil and lemon juice.

TUNA BANH MI
Toss tuna in oil (drained) with lime juice, fish sauce and minced jalapeño. Season with salt and pepper. Spread a split and toasted baguette with mayo; fill with the tuna salad, mint leaves, julienned carrots and sliced dill pickles.

BREADSTICK TWISTS

Active 45 min; Total 1 hr 10 min; Makes about 18 breadsticks

2 cups all-purpose flour

½ tsp. baking powder

1½ tsp. kosher salt, plus more for sprinkling

3 Tbsp. cold unsalted butter, cut into ½-inch pieces

½ cup plus 1 Tbsp. ice water

Extra-virgin olive oil, for brushing

1. Preheat the oven to 375°. In a food processor, pulse the flour with the baking powder and 1½ teaspoons of salt. Add the butter and pulse until the mixture resembles small peas. With the machine on, add the ice water and process just until the dough comes together.

2. Transfer the dough to a lightly floured work surface and pat it into a 1-inch-thick rectangle. Roll out the dough to a 10-by-12-inch rectangle about ¼ inch thick. Cut the dough crosswise into ¼-inch-thick strips.

3. Gently roll each strip into a 14-inch-long stick. Brush 1 stick with water and twist it with another stick, pressing at the top and the bottom. Arrange the twists on a baking sheet. Repeat with the remaining sticks.

4. Brush the twists with olive oil and sprinkle with salt. Bake for about 25 minutes, until golden. Let cool before serving. —*Susan Spungen*

VARIATION To make flavored breadstick twists, add 2 tablespoons of fennel seeds, 2 teaspoons of smoked sweet paprika or 2 teaspoons of curry powder to the flour.

GOLDEN GAZPACHO WITH AVOCADO

Active 15 min; Total 45 min; Serves 4

2 lbs. yellow or orange cherry tomatoes, halved

1 small garlic clove, crushed

¼ cup extra-virgin olive oil

1 jalapeño, seeded and minced

Kosher salt and pepper

Diced avocado and tortilla chips, for serving

In a blender, puree the halved tomatoes and crushed garlic with ¼ cup of water. With the machine on, gradually add the olive oil until incorporated. Transfer to a bowl, stir in the jalapeño and season with salt and pepper. Refrigerate until chilled, about 30 minutes. Ladle the gazpacho into bowls and top with diced avocado. Serve with tortilla chips or breadsticks. —*Justin Chapple*

MAKE AHEAD The gazpacho can be refrigerated overnight.

Suggested Pairing

Offer a crisp, medium-bodied Languedoc white with the tuna noodle dish.

Swordfish Skewers
+ Lemon Brown Rice
+ Avocado-and-Onion Salad

Start the meal with a Cuban-inspired avocado salad from chef Lourdes Castro that is dressed simply with red wine vinegar and olive oil. For the main course, chef Chad Colby uses fresh bay leaves on these swordfish skewers, which impart a lovely fragrance to the dish. Serve the grilled seafood skewers with a lemony brown rice from Emily Farris that can be served warm or chilled.

SWORDFISH SKEWERS WITH SALSA VERDE
Active 45 min; Total 1 hr 45 min; Serves 4

1 cup flat-leaf parsley leaves

10 garlic cloves, crushed

1 tsp. crushed red pepper

½ cup extra-virgin olive oil

Salt and freshly ground black pepper

28 fresh bay leaves (1 cup)

1½ lbs. swordfish, cut into 1½-inch pieces

1 medium zucchini, very thinly sliced lengthwise on a mandoline

2 lemons, halved crosswise

1. In a blender or mini food processor, pulse the parsley, garlic, crushed red pepper and olive oil to a thick puree. Season with salt and pepper and transfer to a bowl.

2. Onto each of 4 long skewers, alternately thread the bay leaves, swordfish and folded zucchini ribbons, repeating until each skewer has 3 pieces of fish, 3 slices of zucchini and 7 bay leaves. Season the skewers with salt and pepper and brush all over with the parsley sauce. Cover and refrigerate for 1 hour.

3. Light a grill or preheat a grill pan. Grill the skewers over moderate heat, turning, until the fish is lightly browned and cooked through, about 6 minutes. Transfer to a platter. Meanwhile, grill the lemon halves, cut side down, until charred, about 2 minutes. Serve the skewers with the grilled lemons. Discard the bay leaves. —*Chad Colby*

How to Throw an Easy Kebab Party

Food writer and editor Tina Ujlaki has a sneaky party strategy: She sets out chunks of meat, poultry, fish and vegetables, then lets guests make and grill their own kebabs.

"When I want to entertain outdoors in the summer but don't feel like standing over a hot grill, I throw a kebab party. I start with quick-cooking cuts of meat, poultry and fish (beef and pork tenderloin, chicken breasts, salmon fillet), plus grill-friendly vegetables, then slice them into pieces of equal thickness. I mix up a few flavorful oils to brush on the kebabs before grilling and sauces to serve with them afterward. Then I let my guests do the rest of the work, assembling their own kebabs, double-skewering ingredients (so they lie flat without spinning) and grilling them. Best of all, to my friends it's not work—it's pure pleasure."

LEMON BROWN RICE WITH GARLIC AND THYME

Active 15 min; Total 1 hr 15 min; Serves 4 to 6

2 Tbsp. unsalted butter

1 shallot, finely chopped

1½ cups short-grain brown rice

3 cups vegetable stock

¼ tsp. kosher salt, plus more for seasoning

¼ tsp. freshly ground pepper plus more for seasoning

2 Tbsp. extra-virgin olive oil

1 Tbsp. garlic, minced

2 Tbsp. chopped thyme

½ tsp. red chili flakes

2 Tbsp. fresh lemon juice

Zest of one lemon

1. In a large saucepan, melt the butter. Add the shallot and cook over moderate heat, stirring occasionally until softened, about 5 minutes. Add the rice and cook, stirring, for 3 minutes. Add the stock, ¼ teaspoon salt and ¼ teaspoon pepper and bring to a boil. Cover and simmer over low heat until the broth is absorbed and the rice is tender, about 45 minutes. Remove from the heat and let stand, covered, for 10 minutes. Fluff with a fork.

2. In a skillet, heat the oil, garlic, thyme and chili flakes over moderately low heat. Cook until garlic is just beginning to brown, about 3 minutes.

3. Remove from heat and add the lemon juice and zest. Season with additional salt and pepper. Toss with cooked rice and serve. —*Emily Farris*

NOTE If eating a gluten-free diet, be sure to use gluten-free stock.

AVOCADO-AND-ONION SALAD

Total 10 min; Serves 4 to 6

1 Florida avocado or 3 Hass avocados, thinly sliced

¼ small red onion, very thinly sliced

1 Tbsp. extra-virgin olive oil

1 Tbsp. red wine vinegar

Salt and freshly ground pepper

Arrange the avocado slices on a platter and top with the onion. Drizzle with the olive oil and vinegar and season with salt and pepper. Serve right away. —*Lourdes Castro*

Suggested Pairing

Herby, citrusy Vermentino from Italy's Ligurian coast was practically made for the swordfish.

Gingery Chicken Satay
+ Coconut Jasmine Rice
+ Sesame Cucumbers

In this ingenious version of an Indonesian classic, the gingery, lemongrass-scented satay paste is the base for the chicken marinade as well as for the luxurious peanut dipping sauce. If you don't want to use chicken, substitute thinly sliced beef or pork or whole, shelled shrimp. Serve with jasmine rice and pickled cucumbers.

Suggested Pairing

Offer a light, fruity Italian Dolcetto from the Piedmont region with the chicken satay.

Indonesian Essentials

If you love Indonesian cuisine, here are some frequently used ingredients that you'll want to keep on hand.

Coconut Milk With its delicate tropical flavor and creamy texture, coconut milk is a popular go-to item for cooks who love Indonesian foods. Despite the name, canned coconut milk is not a dairy product—it comes from the grated meat of the coconut.

Cilantro Also known as Chinese parsley, this herb has wide, lacy green leaves and a pungent flavor. The seed of the cilantro plant is known as coriander. Although cilantro and coriander come from the same plant, their flavors are very different and cannot be substituted for each other.

Fish Sauce Because of its sodium, a little bit of sweetness and a lot of umami, Chef Andy Ricker says that you can think of fish sauce as a liquid form of anchovy. Just a small amount adds a big pop of flavor.

Fresh Ginger This knobby root is aromatic, pungent and spicy and adds its special peppery flavor to Indonesian dishes. Although the flavor can be significantly different, you can use ⅛ teaspoon of ground ginger in place of one tablespoon grated fresh ginger.

Lemongrass It looks a bit like scallions and smells a bit like lemon, but delicately flavored, gently aromatic lemongrass is unique. Cut off the root and the upper two-thirds of the stalk. What's remaining contains the bulb. Peel the outer leaves of the lemongrass stalk—usually just one or two layers—to reveal the bulb. The bulb is usually minced, sliced or crushed before it's added to a dish.

Soy Sauce This sauce is a by-product of fermented soybeans and wheat mixed with brine. The result is an assertive, salty flavor that can be used in marinades, dipping sauces, stir-fries and fried rice. There a number of different types that vary widely in flavor, texture and appearance.

GINGERY CHICKEN SATAY WITH PEANUT SAUCE
Total 30 min; Serves 6

4 large shallots

4 large garlic cloves

2 stalks of lemongrass, bottom 6 inches only, outer leaves peeled, inner stalk cut into 1-inch pieces

2 serrano or jalapeño chiles, stemmed and seeded

2 Tbsp. minced peeled fresh ginger

1 Tbsp. soy sauce

1 tsp. ground coriander

1 tsp. freshly ground pepper

3 Tbsp. light brown sugar

2 Tbsp. Asian fish sauce

2 lbs. skinless, boneless chicken breasts, sliced lengthwise 1 inch thick

3 Tbsp. vegetable oil

1 cup unsweetened coconut milk

½ cup creamy peanut butter

2 Tbsp. fresh lime juice

2 Tbsp. chopped cilantro

1. Light a grill. In a mini food processor, combine the shallots, garlic, lemongrass, chiles, ginger, soy sauce, coriander and ground pepper. Add 2 tablespoons of the brown sugar and 1 tablespoon of the fish sauce and process to a fine paste. Transfer half of the seasoning paste to a large bowl, add the chicken and toss to coat.

2. Thread the chicken strips onto skewers. Drizzle with 2 tablespoons of the vegetable oil and let stand for 10 minutes.

3. Meanwhile, heat the remaining 1 tablespoon of oil in a medium saucepan. Add the remaining seasoning paste and cook over moderate heat, stirring, until fragrant, about 1 minute. Add the coconut milk and bring to a boil, stirring. Whisk in the peanut butter and the remaining 1 tablespoon each of brown sugar and fish sauce and bring to a simmer. Transfer the sauce to a blender, add the lime juice and puree until smooth. Transfer to a bowl.

4. Grill the chicken skewers over a hot fire until lightly charred and cooked through, about 5 minutes. Transfer the chicken to a platter or bowl and sprinkle with the cilantro. Serve with the peanut sauce. —*Grace Parisi*

COCONUT JASMINE RICE

Total 20 min; Serves 6 to 8

1 cup unsweetened coconut milk

1 tsp. sea salt

2½ cups jasmine rice, rinsed

2 kaffir lime leaves

In a large saucepan, combine the coconut milk and salt with 3 cups of water. Add the rinsed rice and lime leaves and bring to a boil. Cover and simmer over low heat for 12 minutes. Turn off the heat and let the rice stand, covered, for 5 minutes. Fluff the rice, discard the lime leaves and serve.

TAIWANESE SESAME CUCUMBERS

Total 25 min; Serves 6

2 seedless cucumbers, chilled in the freezer for 10 minutes

¼ cup toasted sesame oil

3 Tbsp. rice vinegar

Kosher salt

¼ cup sesame seeds

¼ tsp. crushed red pepper

2 scallions, coarsely chopped

1. Cut the cucumbers lengthwise into eighths, then cut them crosswise into 2-inch-long sticks. In a large bowl, combine the sesame oil, vinegar and a large pinch of salt. Add the cucumbers and toss well. Let stand for 10 minutes, tossing a few times.

2. In a mini food processor, combine the sesame seeds, crushed red pepper and 1½ teaspoons of salt. Process until the sesame seeds are coarsely chopped. Add half of the mixture to the cucumbers and toss well. Arrange cucumbers on a platter. Sprinkle with the remaining sesame seed mixture and the scallions and serve.

—*Joanne Chang*

+BONUS RECIPE: DESSERT
COCONUT CRÈME CARAMEL

Active: 25 min; Total: 1 hr 45 min plus overnight chilling
Serves 8 to 10

1 cup granulated sugar

¼ cup water

10 large egg yolks

¾ cup light brown sugar

2 cups heavy cream

One 13-oz. can unsweetened coconut milk

1½ teaspoons pure vanilla extract

Pinch of salt

½ cup sweetened shredded coconut, toasted

1. Preheat the oven to 350°. In a saucepan, cook the granulated sugar with the water over moderate heat, brushing down the sides of the pan with a wet brush, until a rich amber caramel forms, about 15 minutes. Quickly pour the caramel into a 9-inch square glass or ceramic baking dish to coat the bottom.

2. In a bowl, beat the egg yolks and brown sugar until very thick, 2 minutes. Beat in the cream, coconut milk, vanilla and salt and pour into the baking dish. Set the dish in a roasting pan. Pour hot water in the pan to come halfway up the dish's side. Bake for 1 hour, until the custard is just set but still jiggly in the center. Refrigerate in the dish overnight.

3. Run a knife around the edge of the custard. Set the dish in a pan of hot water for 10 seconds. Invert a flat platter over the dish, then turn the custard and caramel onto the platter. Top with the toasted coconut and serve. —*Zang Too*

Chipotle Chicken Tacos
+ Grilled Vegetables
+ Chile-and-Mango Guacamole

These super easy chicken tacos from chef Alex Stupak are packed with tasty shredded thigh meat, tomatoes and spicy jalapeños. Instead of playing the supporting role as a side dish, the grilled vegetables from Grace Parisi are more of a co-star in this casual summer menu. Fresno chiles are similar in shape and heat to jalapeños, but they're red and a little less meaty. Roasting them over a flame tames their spice and brings out their natural sweetness. Round out the menu with chef Steve Minter's Mango Guacamole.

CHIPOTLE CHICKEN TACOS
Active 30 min; Total 1 hr 15 min; Serves 4

8 chicken thighs (3 lbs.)

2 Tbsp. vegetable oil, plus more for brushing

Salt and pepper

½ medium white onion, minced, plus more for serving

2 jalapeños, stemmed, seeded and minced

2 Tbsp. minced chipotle chiles, plus 3 Tbsp. adobo sauce from the can or jar

4 plum tomatoes, finely chopped

Warm corn tortillas, cilantro leaves, sour cream and lime wedges, for serving

1. Preheat the oven to 350°. On a large rimmed baking sheet, brush the chicken with oil and season with salt and pepper. Bake for about 45 minutes, until an instant-read thermometer inserted in the largest piece registers 165°. Let cool, then shred the meat; discard the skin and bones.

2. In a large skillet, heat the 2 tablespoons of oil until shimmering. Add the ½ onion, the jalapeños and a generous pinch of salt and cook over moderate heat, stirring occasionally, until just softened, about 5 minutes. Add the chipotles and adobo sauce and cook for 2 minutes. Add the tomatoes and cook until softened and any liquid has evaporated, about 7 minutes. Stir in the shredded chicken and cook until hot, about 3 minutes. Season with salt and pepper.

3. Spoon the chicken into warm corn tortillas and serve with cilantro, sour cream, lime wedges and minced onion.
—*Alex Stupak*

6 Delicious Upgrades for Chicken Tacos

FRIED CHICKEN Chef Andrew Zimmern stuffs his tacos with extra-crispy fried skin-on boneless chicken thighs. He tops them with little more than an avocado-tomatillo salsa.

GRILLED SCALLIONS Give tacos a springy kick with smoky scallions. When grilled, they become extra sweet and silky.

AVOCADO CREMA Instead of the traditional crema, try blending avocado with thick and creamy nonfat Greek yogurt.

ASIAN STYLE Replace the tortillas with sheets of nori and top the chicken with kimchi mayonnaise, sesame seeds and a drizzle of teriyaki.

BARBECUE CHICKEN Sweet and smoky barbecue sauce is an easy way to change up chicken tacos. Try topping the saucy meat with crunchy cabbage slaw.

SPICY BLACK BEANS Simmered black beans are terrific with pulled chicken, avocado and cilantro.

GRILLED VEGETABLES WITH ROASTED-CHILE BUTTER

Total 35 min; Serves 4

3 red Fresno chiles or jalapeños

¼ tsp. minced Scotch Bonnet chile or ¼ tsp. cayenne pepper

½ stick unsalted butter, softened

1 Tbsp. minced chives

¼ lb. King Oyster or portobello mushrooms, sliced lengthwise ⅝ inch thick

½ lb. Japanese eggplants or baby eggplants, sliced on the diagonal ⅝ inch thick

½ lb. small zucchini (about 2), thinly sliced on the diagonal

1 ear of corn, shucked, cobs cut crosswise into 1½-inch-thick rounds

Extra-virgin olive oil, for grilling

Salt and freshly ground black pepper

1. Light a grill or preheat a grill pan. Grill the Fresno chiles over high heat, turning, until blackened and softened, 4 to 5 minutes. Transfer the chiles to a bowl, cover with plastic wrap and let cool slightly. Peel, seed and mince the chiles

and return them to the bowl. Add the Scotch Bonnet, butter and chives and stir until combined.

2. Lightly brush the mushrooms, eggplant, zucchini and corn with olive oil and season with salt and pepper. Grill the vegetables over moderately high heat, turning once or twice, until lightly charred and tender, about 5 minutes. Arrange the vegetables on a platter and immediately dot with the chile butter. Serve right away. *—Grace Parisi*

SMOKED-CHILE-AND-MANGO GUACAMOLE

Total 20 min; Makes 2½ cups

1 Tbsp. extra-virgin olive oil

2 plum tomatoes, cut into ¼-inch dice

1 shallot, finely chopped

2 dried chipotle chiles, stems discarded and chiles finely crushed

Kosher salt

2 Hass avocados, halved, pitted and diced

½ cup finely chopped white onion

1 serrano chile, minced

3 Tbsp. fresh lime juice

½ mango, cut into ¼-inch dice (½ cup)

1 cup lightly packed cilantro, finely chopped, plus whole leaves, for garnish

Tortilla chips, for serving

1. In a medium skillet, heat the olive oil. Stir in half of the diced plum tomatoes and add shallot, crushed chipotles and a generous pinch of salt and cook over moderate heat, stirring occasionally, until chiles are softened, about 5 minutes. Scrape mixture into a large bowl; cool completely.

2. Add avocados, onion, serrano chile, lime juice and remaining diced tomato to the bowl and stir gently. Gently fold in diced mango and 1 cup of chopped cilantro and season with salt. Garnish with cilantro leaves and serve with tortilla chips. *—Steve Minter*

Suggested Pairing

Pair the tacos with ice-cold canned Mexican lager.

Arroz Con Pollo
+ Summer Salad with Herbs
+ Avocado–Green Pea Salsa

Using a family recipe, chef Jose Enrique makes this chicken-and-rice dish with what seems like too much stock, wine and pilsner, but the result is an exceptionally moist dish. Using a short-grain rice such as Bomba helps absorb the liquid. Serve the chicken dish with a colorful salsa that combines green peas and creamy diced avocado with a hit of lime and round out the menu with a crisp summertime green salad from Kay Chun.

ARROZ CON POLLO
Active 1 hr; Total 1 hr 15 min; Serves 4

2 Tbsp. extra-virgin olive oil

One 3½-lb. chicken, cut into 8 pieces

Kosher salt and pepper

1 medium onion, minced

2 serrano chiles, seeded and minced

2 garlic cloves, minced

3 plum tomatoes (1 lb.), cored and finely diced

1 tsp. ground achiote (annatto)

½ tsp. ground cumin

Small pinch of saffron threads

1 cup dry white wine

3 cups chicken stock

1 cup pilsner or light beer

2 cups Bomba or other short-grain rice

½ cup chopped parsley

Avocado-Green Pea Salsa, for serving

JE Hot Sauce or other hot sauce, for serving

1. Preheat the oven to 400°. In a very large, deep ovenproof skillet, heat the olive oil until shimmering. Season the chicken with salt and pepper. Cook skin side down over moderate heat, turning once, until nicely browned, 10 to 12 minutes. Transfer to a plate.

2. Add the onion, serranos and garlic to the skillet and season with a generous pinch each of salt and pepper. Cook over moderately high heat, stirring occasionally, until softened, about 6 minutes. Add the tomatoes, achiote, cumin and saffron and cook, stirring, until the tomatoes start to break down, about 5 minutes. Add the wine and simmer until slightly reduced, about 3 minutes. Add the stock and beer and bring to a boil. Stir in the rice and return to a boil. Nestle the chicken into the rice and bake uncovered in the lower third of the oven for about 30 minutes, until the liquid is absorbed, the rice is tender and the chicken is cooked through.

3. Transfer the chicken to a plate. Fluff the rice with a fork, then gently fold in the parsley and season with salt and pepper. Return the chicken to the skillet and serve with Avocado-Green Pea Salsa and hot sauce. —*Jose Enrique*

SUMMER SALAD WITH HERBS AND PITA CRISPS

Total 40 min; Serves 4 to 6

6 Tbsp. extra-virgin olive oil, plus more for brushing

1 tsp. finely grated garlic

2 pita breads, each split into 2 rounds

Kosher salt and pepper

½ lb. haricots verts, green beans or wax beans, trimmed

1 mint sprig, plus 2 cups chopped mint

2 Tbsp. fresh lemon juice

1 shallot, minced

1 Kirby cucumber, chopped

6 cups packed chopped baby romaine (6 oz.)

2 cups parsley leaves

12 multicolored cherry tomatoes, halved

1 cup sunflower sprouts or chopped purslane

1. Preheat the oven to 375°. In a small bowl, mix the 6 tablespoons of olive oil with the garlic. Brush the pita with 2 tablespoons of the garlic oil. Toast in the oven for 5 to 7 minutes, until crisp and golden. Transfer the pita to a plate; season with salt and pepper. Let cool, then break into big crisps.

2. Meanwhile, in a medium saucepan of salted boiling water, blanch the beans until crisp-tender, about 2 minutes. Drain and chill in a bowl of ice water. Drain and pat dry; halve the beans crosswise.

3. Rub the mint sprig all over the inside of a large wooden bowl; discard the sprig. In the bowl, mix the remaining 4 tablespoons of garlic oil with the lemon juice and shallot; season with salt and pepper. Add the chopped mint, beans, cucumber, romaine, parsley, tomatoes, sprouts and pita crisps and toss to evenly coat. —*Kay Chun*

AVOCADO-GREEN PEA SALSA

Total 25 min; Serves 4

1 cup fresh or thawed frozen peas

1 small red onion, minced

¼ cup fresh lime juice

Kosher salt

3 Hass avocados, peeled, pitted and finely diced

¼ cup extra-virgin olive oil

1. In a medium saucepan of salted boiling water, blanch the peas until crisp-tender, about 1 minute. Drain and cool under running water, then drain on paper towels.

2. In a bowl, mix the onion with the lime juice and ¾ teaspoon of salt; let stand for 10 minutes. Fold in the avocados, peas and oil, season with salt and serve. —*Jose Enrique*

MAKE AHEAD The salsa can be refrigerated overnight.

+BONUS RECIPE: COCKTAIL
WHITE SANGRIA

Total 10 min plus chilling; Makes 6 drinks

One 750-ml. bottle rich white wine, such as Chardonnay

4 oz. brandy

2 oz. simple syrup

1 cup mixed chunks of seeded oranges, lemon and limes

Combine all ingredients in a pitcher. Refrigerate until the drink is chilled and the flavors are blended, about 4 to 8 hours. Serve the sangria with ice in chilled wineglasses. —*Bridget Albert*

NOTE To make simple syrup, simmer ½ cup water with ½ cup sugar in a small saucepan over moderate heat, stirring until the sugar has dissolved. Let the syrup cool.

Summer Salad with Herbs
and Pita Crisps

Bacon-and-Kimchi Burgers
+ Sweet Potato Chips
+ Cucumber–Sugar Snap Salad

Elevate burger night with chef Wesley Genovart's over-the-top burger featuring two thin-stacked patties, thick-cut bacon, kimchi and a spicy homemade sauce. Balance out the flavors of the burger with a tangy salad that combines cucumbers with sugar snaps in a yogurt dressing and an unexpected crunchy granola topping. And don't forget the chips: These addictive homemade sweet potato chips are easy to make and impossible to resist.

BACON-AND-KIMCHI BURGERS

Total 30 min; Serves 4

¼ cup sambal oelek (Indonesian chile sauce)

¼ cup mayonnaise

¼ cup ketchup

4 slices of thick-cut bacon

1¼ lbs. ground beef chuck

Kosher salt

4 slices of American cheese

4 potato buns, toasted

1 cup chopped drained cabbage kimchi (6 oz.)

1. In a small bowl, combine the sambal with the mayonnaise and ketchup and mix well.

2. Light a grill or preheat a grill pan. Grill the bacon over moderate heat, turning, until golden and crisp, about 5 minutes total. Drain on paper towels.

3. Form the beef into eight ¼-inch-thick burgers and season with salt. Grill over high heat, turning, until browned, 1 minute per side. Make 4 stacks of 2 burgers each on the grill and spoon 1 tablespoon of the sambal mayo over each stack. Top with the cheese, cover and grill over high heat just until the cheese is melted, about 1 minute.

4. Spread the remaining sambal mayo on the bottom buns. Top with the burgers, bacon and kimchi, close and serve.
—Wesley Genovart

4 Tips to Achieving Burger Greatness

GET THE RIGHT BUN Seattle chef Josh Henderson is obsessed with burger buns and one day hopes to create his own perfect "dive-bar bun" with quality ingredients. One of his perfect bun criteria: "When you squeeze a burger bun, it shouldn't bounce back, it should adhere to the burger," he says.

GIVE YOUR PATTY A QUICK DIP "Some chefs will say this is crazy," says chef Laurent Tourondel, "but you can make a burger juicier by dunking the patty in cold water for about 30 seconds before grilling." The technique prevents the fat from melting before the meat hits the grill, which can make for a tough burger.

BE HANDS-OFF Burger purists like Adam Fleischman of Umami Burger handle the ground meat as little as possible. Overworking the patty can create a meatloaf-like texture.

BASTE YOUR BURGER Chef Tourondel also brushes burgers with butter while they're on the grill. The natural sugars caramelize, making the meat extra-delicious.

CUCUMBER-SUGAR SNAP SALAD

Total 15 min; Serves 4

3 Tbsp. extra-virgin olive oil

3 Tbsp. fat-free plain Greek yogurt

Salt and pepper

1 hothouse cucumber, cut crosswise into thirds and julienned

¼ lb. sugar snap peas, thinly sliced

Nutty granola, for garnish

In a large bowl, whisk the olive oil with the yogurt and 1 tablespoon of water. Season with salt and pepper. Add the cucumbers and sugar snaps and toss to coat. Transfer the salad to plates and top with granola. —KC

+BONUS RECIPE: DESSERT

CREAMY MOCHA ICE POPS

Active 25 min; Total 25 min plus 6 hr chilling time
Makes 10

2½ oz. dark chocolate, finely chopped

½ cup plus 1 Tbsp. sugar

½ cup ground medium-roast coffee (3 oz.)

1 cup heavy cream

Chopped toasted hazelnuts (optional)

1. Line a sieve with cheesecloth. Put the chocolate in a heatproof bowl. In a medium saucepan, combine ½ cup of the sugar with the coffee and 1¾ cups of water and bring to a boil. Simmer over low heat for 4 minutes, stirring. Strain the coffee in the cheesecloth-lined sieve over the chocolate; whisk until melted. Let cool, then refrigerate for at least 2 hours or overnight.

2. In a medium bowl, using a hand mixer, beat the cream with the remaining sugar at medium speed until soft peaks form. Whisk the chilled mixture until smooth, then fold in the whipped cream. Pour the mocha mixture into the ice pop molds; freeze for at least 4 hours. If using hazelnuts, press the frozen ice pops into the chopped nuts and return to the freezer for at least 30 minutes before serving.
—Gabriele Corcos

BAKED SWEET POTATO CHIPS

Active 15 min; Total 1 hr; Makes 3 cups

1 small sweet potato (8 oz.), peeled and thinly sliced on a mandoline ⅛ inch thick

3 Tbsp. extra-virgin olive oil

Kosher salt and pepper

Preheat the oven to 275°. Set a rack on each of 2 baking sheets. In a bowl, toss the sweet potato slices with the oil and season with salt and pepper; make sure each slice is coated with oil. Arrange the slices in a single layer on the racks. Bake for 45 to 50 minutes, rotating the sheets halfway through baking, until the chips are deeply golden. The chips will crisp as they cool. —Kay Chun

MAKE AHEAD The chips can be stored overnight in an airtight container.

Suggested Pairing

Pair the juicy burgers with a hoppy, but balanced New England IPA.

Sausage Burgers
+ Grilled Potato Salad
+ Corn on the Cob

Chef Donald Link got the inspiration for this robust sausage burger from Cajun and Creole cooking and it's prodigious use of tomatoes and green peppers. Serve the burgers with summertime classics—grilled corn and potato salad. Marcia Kiesel's grilled corn on the cob is accented with a trio of salts and Stephanie Izard's grilled potato salad is dressed with a tangy mustard vinaigrette.

SAUSAGE BURGERS WITH GRILLED GREEN CHILES

Total 1 hr; Serves 6

2½ lbs. ground pork

2 Tbsp. minced garlic, plus 4 garlic cloves, thinly sliced

2 Tbsp. balsamic vinegar

1 tsp. crushed red pepper

1 tsp. chopped thyme

Kosher salt and freshly ground pepper

5 large fresh Anaheim chiles

1 large poblano chile

2 Tbsp. extra-virgin olive oil

½ tsp. chopped rosemary

6 oz. Gruyère or Italian Fontina cheese, cut into 6 slices about ¼ inch thick

6 ciabatta or kaiser rolls, split and lightly toasted

¼ cup plus 2 Tbsp. whole-grain or Dijon mustard

2 cups arugula leaves

1 large Creole tomato (see Note) or beefsteak tomato, cut into 6 slices

1. In a large bowl, gently mix the ground pork with the minced garlic, balsamic vinegar, crushed red pepper, thyme, 1 tablespoon of kosher salt and 2 teaspoons of black pepper. Pat the meat into 6 burgers, cover with plastic wrap and refrigerate.

2. Light a grill. Grill the Anaheim and poblano chiles over a hot fire, turning, until charred all over. Transfer to a bowl, cover with plastic wrap and let steam for 10 minutes. Peel, stem and seed the chiles, then cut them into long, thin strips. Transfer the chiles to a bowl and add the olive oil, rosemary and sliced garlic. Season with salt and pepper.

3. Grill the burgers over a hot fire until just cooked through, about 5 minutes per side. About 1 minute before the burgers are done, place a slice of cheese on each burger.

4. Spread the bottom half of each roll with 1 tablespoon of mustard. Top with the arugula and a tomato slice. Set the burgers on the tomato slices and cover with the marinated chiles. Close the sandwiches and serve. —*Donald Link*

MAKE AHEAD The uncooked burgers and marinated chiles can be refrigerated overnight.

NOTE Creole tomatoes are a large, juicy, bright red variety of tomato grown in the hot and humid Mississippi Delta region of Louisiana. These tomatoes have a lower acid content and meatier texture than most other tomatoes.

GRILLED POTATO SALAD WITH MUSTARD SEEDS

Total 50 min; Serves 6

4 large Kennebec or baking potatoes, cut into ½-inch-thick rounds

Salt and pepper

1 stick unsalted butter

3 Tbsp. seasoned rice vinegar

2 Tbsp. mustard seeds

¼ cup sherry vinegar

2 tsp. pure maple syrup

2 tsp. fresh lemon juice

¼ cup rice bran or canola oil

2 celery ribs, thinly sliced

4 scallions, thinly sliced

1. In a large saucepan, cover the potato rounds with water and bring to a boil. Add a generous pinch of salt and simmer over moderate heat until the potatoes are tender but not falling apart, about 12 minutes. Drain and transfer to a baking sheet to cool.

2. Light a grill or preheat a grill pan. Lay 2 large sheets of heavy-duty foil on a work surface. Fold up the edges to form a ½-inch rim and pinch the corners together to seal. Transfer the foil to the grill and melt the butter on it. Add the potatoes in a single layer and grill over moderate heat until browned on the bottom, 12 to 15 minutes.

3. Meanwhile, in a small saucepan, bring the rice vinegar just to a boil. Add the mustard seeds and let cool completely. Whisk in the sherry vinegar, maple syrup, lemon juice and rice bran oil. Season the dressing with salt and pepper.

4. Transfer potatoes to a large bowl. Add celery, scallions and dressing; gently toss to coat. Season with salt and pepper and toss again. —*Stephanie Izard*

CORN ON THE COB WITH SEASONED SALTS

Total 30 min; Serves 4

1½ Tbsp. Maldon or Halen Môn Welsh sea salt

2 tsp. finely grated orange zest

1½ Tbsp. kosher salt

1 tsp. hot smoked paprika

1½ Tbsp. coarse smoked salt

1 Tbsp. coarsely ground black pepper

8 ears of corn, shucked

Vegetable oil, for drizzling

Unsalted butter, for serving

1. Prepare the salts in 3 small bowls: Mix the Maldon salt with the orange zest, the kosher salt with the paprika and the smoked salt with the black pepper.

2. Light a grill. Drizzle the corn with vegetable oil and rub to coat the corn thoroughly. Grill over moderate heat, turning often, until the corn is lightly charred all over and just tender, about 15 minutes. Transfer the corn to a large platter and serve with butter and the seasoned salts. —*Marcia Kiesel*

Suggested Pairing

Pair the burgers with a berry-inflected Zinfandel or a yeasty pilsner.

Roast Beef Summer Rolls
+ Vietnamese-Style Shrimp
+ Carrot and Daikon Pickles

Vietnamese summer rolls are often filled with pork or shrimp, but Grace Parisi makes hers with roast beef from the deli. Use shrimp instead in chef Steven Raichlen's shrimp skewered with sugarcane, which flavors the shrimp from the inside out. Serve with a jar of carrot and daikon pickles from Marcia Kiesel.

ROAST BEEF SUMMER ROLLS

Total 40 min; Serves 6

1 large garlic clove, smashed

1½ Tbsp. light brown sugar

1 tsp. Thai green curry paste

2 Tbsp. fresh lime juice

2 Tbsp. Asian fish sauce

¼ cup chopped cilantro

¼ cup chopped mint

⅓ cup mayonnaise

4 cups coleslaw mix

½ lb. rare deli roast beef, thinly sliced and cut into ½-inch strips

24 six-inch-round rice paper wrappers, plus more in case of breakage

1. In a mortar, pound the garlic to a paste with the brown sugar and green curry paste. Add the lime juice, fish sauce and 3 tablespoons of water. Stir in half of the cilantro and mint. In a small bowl, whisk the mayonnaise with 1 tablespoon of the green curry dipping sauce.

2. In a large bowl, toss the coleslaw mix with the roast beef and the remaining cilantro and mint.

3. Fill a pie plate with warm water. Dip 2 or 3 rice paper wrappers at a time in the water, then set them on a work surface to soften, about 1 minute. Spread a scant teaspoon of the curry mayonnaise on the bottom third of each wrapper and top with a scant 3 tablespoons of the roast beef filling. Roll the wrappers into tight cylinders, tucking in the sides as you go. Transfer the rolls to a plastic wrap–lined baking sheet and repeat with the remaining wrappers, curry mayonnaise and filling.

4. Just before serving, cut each roll in half and serve with the dipping sauce. —*Grace Parisi*

Suggested Pairing

Try a Rhône-style white from California's central coast with the herby summer rolls.

VIETNAMESE-STYLE JUMBO SHRIMP ON SUGARCANE

Active 40 min; Total 1 hr 10 min plus 2 hr marinating time
Serves 6

4 garlic cloves, coarsely chopped

⅓ cup sugar, divided

2 large shallots, coarsely chopped

½ cup Asian fish sauce, divided

¼ cup plus 3 Tbsp. fresh lime juice, divided

1 tsp. freshly ground pepper

3 stalks of fresh lemongrass, tender inner white bulbs only, thinly sliced crosswise

¼ cup vegetable oil, plus more for brushing

24 jumbo shrimp, shelled and deveined

VIETNAMESE DIPPING SAUCE

One 2-inch piece carrot

2 garlic cloves, minced

½ cup warm water

2 Tbsp. white vinegar

1 red Thai chile, thinly sliced

12 sugarcane swizzle sticks (see Note)

3 Tbsp. chopped peanuts

3 Tbsp. coarsely chopped cilantro

1. In a food processor, combine chopped garlic, 3 tablespoons sugar, shallots, ¼ cup fish sauce, 3 tablespoons lime juice and pepper. Add lemongrass and ¼ cup vegetable oil; process to a puree. Arrange shrimp in a large, shallow glass dish in a single layer; pour marinade on top. Turn shrimp to coat thoroughly. Cover and refrigerate 2 hours.

2. Make the dipping sauce Slice carrot lengthwise with a sturdy vegetable peeler. Stack the slices and cut lengthwise into very fine julienne strips. In a bowl, mash 2 minced garlic cloves with 2 tablespoons sugar. Add ½ cup warm water, ¼ cup Asian fish sauce, ¼ cup fresh lime juice, white vinegar, chile and carrots and stir well.

3. Light a grill. Cut each sugarcane stick in half on a sharp diagonal so each piece has a sharp point. Scrape off most of the marinade from the shrimp. Working with the shrimp's natural curl, use a small, sharp knife to make 2 slits—one near the tail end and one near the head. Thread a sugarcane stick through the slits; the shrimp should lie flat. Repeat with the remaining shrimp.

4. Grill the shrimp over a hot fire, brushing them once or twice with oil, until lightly charred and just cooked through, about 3 minutes per side. Transfer the shrimp to a platter and sprinkle the peanuts and cilantro on top. Serve the shrimp with the Vietnamese Dipping Sauce. —*Steven Raichlen*

MAKE AHEAD The lemongrass marinade can be refrigerated overnight.

NOTE Sugarcane swizzle sticks are available in the fruit department of many large supermarkets. Alternatively, look for canned sugarcane in syrup at Asian markets; you'll have to drain the sugarcane and cut it into lengthwise sticks with a sharp knife.

CARROT AND DAIKON PICKLES
Active 15 min; Total 2 hr 15 min; Serves 6

¾ cup white vinegar

2 Tbsp. sugar

2 tsp. kosher salt

3 large carrots, peeled and sliced crosswise ⅛ inch thick

1 lb. daikon, peeled and cut into ½-inch-long matchsticks

In a medium bowl, combine the vinegar, sugar and kosher salt; stir to dissolve the sugar and salt. Add the carrots and daikon. Cover them with a small plate and a heavy can to keep them submerged in the pickling liquid. Let stand at room temperature for 2 hours. —*Marcia Kiesel*

MAKE AHEAD The pickles can be refrigerated for up to 1 week.

How to Roll Perfect Summer Rolls

1. Dip rice paper wrappers in a pie plate or bowl of warm water.

4. Roll once.

2. Let soften on a work surface and mound with fillings on one end.

5. Tuck in the sides of the wrapper.

6. Continue to roll into a tight cylinder. The remaining edge will seal itself.

3. Fold the edge of the wrapper over the filling.

Barbecued Baby Back Ribs
+ Peppered Corn Bread
+ Grilled Tomato Salad

Welcome grilling season with these sticky, apple-scented ribs that are cooked in the oven, then finished on the grill. They're a simpler version of a recipe by champion pit master Chris Lilly, who cooks his ribs entirely on the grill. To follow Lilly's example, use a thermometer to keep the temperature at a steady 250° and wrap the ribs in foil after adding the cider mixture. Use the grill for chef Tim Love's simple tomato salad or serve with a vinegar-dressed coleslaw.

APPLE-GLAZED BARBECUED BABY BACK RIBS

Active 30 min; Total 4 hr 30 min; Serves 4

½ cup packed dark brown sugar

4 tsp. garlic salt

4 tsp. pure ancho chile powder

2 tsp. kosher salt

1 tsp. freshly ground black pepper

½ tsp. celery salt

¼ tsp. cayenne pepper

¼ tsp. ground cinnamon

¼ tsp. freshly ground white pepper

½ cup apple cider

¼ cup apple jelly, melted

¼ cup honey

2 racks baby back ribs (about 4 lbs. total)

1 cup prepared barbecue sauce

1. Preheat the oven to 250°. In a small bowl, mix ¼ cup of the sugar with the garlic salt, chile powder, kosher salt, black pepper, celery salt, cayenne, cinnamon and white pepper. Transfer 1 tablespoon of the spice mix to a medium bowl and whisk in the cider, apple jelly, honey and the remaining ¼ cup of sugar.

2. Working with one rib rack at a time, with the bones facing up, insert a knife at one end between the meat and the membrane. Using the knife, loosen the skin and peel it back until it's fully removed. Discard.

3. On a rimmed baking sheet, rub the ribs with the remaining spice mix; bake, meaty side up, for 2½ hours. Pour the cider mixture over the ribs and turn to coat. Tightly cover with foil and bake for 1 hour longer.

4. Light a grill. Uncover the ribs, brush with the barbecue sauce and grill over moderate heat, turning and brushing, until glazed, about 15 minutes. Let rest for 10 minutes, then cut between the bones and serve. —*Chris Lilly*

How to Remove the Silver Skin from Baby Back Ribs

1. With the bones facing up, insert a knife at one end between the meat and the membrane (silver skin).

2. Using the knife, loosen the skin and peel it back until it's fully removed. Discard.

PEPPERED CORN BREAD

Active 10 min; Total 1 hr; Makes one 10-inch round

Canola oil, for brushing

2 cups stone-ground cornmeal

½ cup all-purpose flour

1 Tbsp. sugar

1 tsp. baking powder

1 tsp. baking soda

1 tsp. kosher salt

1 tsp. freshly ground pepper

2 large eggs, lightly beaten

2 cups buttermilk

½ cup fat-free sour cream

3 Tbsp. unsalted butter, melted

1. Preheat the oven to 375°. Rub a 10-inch cast-iron skillet with oil and heat it in the oven.

2. In a large bowl, whisk the cornmeal with the flour, sugar, baking powder, baking soda, salt and pepper. In a medium bowl, whisk the eggs, buttermilk, sour cream and butter, then whisk into the dry ingredients until combined. Pour the batter into the skillet.

3. Bake the corn bread for about 35 minutes, until risen and golden and a toothpick inserted in the center comes out with a few moist crumbs. Let cool for 20 minutes, cut into wedges and serve. —*John Currence*

Suggested Pairing

The sweet spice of a Syrah from California or Washington state is a good match for the glazed ribs.

GRILLED TOMATO-AND-SCALLION SALAD

Total 20 min; Serves 4 to 6

4 tomatoes (6 to 8 oz. each), cut into 6 wedges

1 bunch of scallions

Canola oil, for rubbing

Kosher salt and freshly ground pepper

2 Tbsp. fresh lime juice

2 Tbsp. extra-virgin olive oil

1 cup crumbled Cotija or ricotta salata cheese (about 2 oz.)

1. Light a grill. Rub the tomatoes and scallions with canola oil and season with salt and pepper. Grill the tomatoes and scallions over high heat, turning once, until they're blistered, 1 minute per side.

2. Transfer to a platter. Drizzle the salad with the lime juice and olive oil, sprinkle with the cheese and serve. —*Tim Love*

T-Bone Steaks
+ Watermelon Salad
+ Grill-Baked Potatoes

Big, thick steaks need a lot of seasoning, so be sure to cover them liberally with salt, pepper and any rub before grilling. Serve the T-bones with super easy, indulgent potatoes based on a recipe from Brooklyn butcher Tom Mylan. They're layered with pats of chive and sour cream butter, then wrapped in foil and grilled until soft and delicious. The watermelon-feta salad, from chef Walker Stern is updated with the addition of smoky charred shishito peppers, fresh herbs and spicy Korean red chile powder.

SPICE-RUBBED T-BONE STEAKS
Total 20 min; Serves 4

2 tsp. ancho chile powder

1½ tsp. ground cumin

1 tsp. hot paprika

1 tsp. garlic powder

Kosher salt and freshly ground pepper

2 T-bone steaks, cut 1-inch thick (3¼ lbs. total), at room temperature

Light a grill. In a small bowl, mix the ancho chile powder, cumin, paprika and garlic powder with 1 tablespoon of salt and 1 teaspoon of pepper. Season the steaks with the spice rub and grill over moderate heat for 8 minutes per side for medium-rare. Transfer to a work surface and let rest for 5 minutes before serving. —Melissa Rubel Jacobson

Suggested Pairing

Serve the steaks with a berry-inflected, peppery Argentinean Malbec.

Steak Tips from the Pros

ON SEASONING
"Use a lot of salt. Everybody underseasons meat. It takes a tremendous amount of salt before it actually becomes well seasoned." — *Grant Achatz, Alinea and Next; Chicago*

ON BEING TOO TOUCHY-FEELY
"I try not to be the chef when I go to a friend's house for a barbecue, but I can't stand it when guys flip the steak a hundred times to get the flames to come up. You should only touch the steak three or four times the whole time you're cooking it, whether it's on the grill or in a pan. There's a lot of juice in there that you don't want to mess with." — *Marc Forgione, American Cut; New York City*

ON KNOWING WHEN IT'S DONE
"Use your thermometer, and know how to calibrate it. There's no shame in a thermometer at all. People will tell you about the trick of testing a steak's doneness by pressing on it and comparing it to the firmness of the flesh of your hand, but all steaks have different muscle fibers, so it doesn't always work." —*John Gorham, Tasty n Alder; Portland, Oregon*

ON SERVING STEAK AT A PARTY "Sear the steaks on the grill or in your cast-iron pan until they're slightly more rare than you want them, and then let them rest at room temperature for up to three or four hours. When you're ready to eat, put them on the top rack in your grill and shut the lid, or pop them in the oven at 450° for just a minute or two, and they'll be ready to serve, right at the temperature where you want them." —*Tim Love, Queenie's; Denton, Texas*

1. In a large glass or ceramic baking dish, gently toss the watermelon, cucumbers, red onion, vinegar, *gochugaru* and ¼ cup of the olive oil. Spread in an even layer and season with salt and pepper.

2. In a large skillet, heat the remaining 2 tablespoons of olive oil until shimmering. Add the shishitos and cook over high heat, tossing, until charred in spots and crisp-tender, about 2 minutes. Transfer the shishitos to the baking dish and toss.

3. Transfer the salad to plates and garnish with the olives, feta, watercress, cilantro and dill. Serve right away.
—*Walker Stern*

GRILL-BAKED POTATOES WITH CHIVE BUTTER

Active 25 min; Total 2 hr 10 min; Serves 4

1 stick unsalted butter, softened

¾ cup finely chopped chives, plus more for garnish

½ cup sour cream, plus more for serving

1½ tsp. kosher salt

1 tsp. freshly ground pepper

Four 10-oz. baking potatoes

1. In a medium bowl, combine the butter, ¾ cup of chives, ½ cup of sour cream and the salt and pepper; mix until smooth. Transfer the butter to a large sheet of plastic wrap and form into a log. Wrap and refrigerate until firm, about 1 hour.

2. Light a grill. Using a sharp knife, slice each potato crosswise at ⅓-inch intervals, cutting down but not all the way through the potato. Cut chive butter into thin slices, then carefully tuck butter in between potato slices. Wrap each potato tightly in aluminum foil.

3. Set the potatoes on the grill over low heat, cover and cook, turning occasionally, until tender, 45 to 50 minutes. Unwrap the potatoes, garnish with finely chopped chives and serve with sour cream. —*Tom Mylan*

MAKE AHEAD The compound butter can be wrapped in plastic and refrigerated for up to 2 days.

WATERMELON, FETA AND CHARRED PEPPER SALAD

Total 30 min; Serves 4 to 6

1 lb. seedless watermelon, cubed (1-inch pieces; from one 3¼-lb. watermelon)

2 Kirby cucumbers, peeled and cut into ¾-inch dice

¼ cup very thinly sliced red onion

1½ Tbsp. sherry vinegar

½ tsp. gochugaru (Korean chile powder) or Aleppo pepper

6 Tbsp. extra-virgin olive oil

Kosher salt and pepper

20 medium shishito peppers (4 oz.)

20 pitted kalamata olives, halved

4 oz. feta, crumbled

1 cup lightly packed watercress leaves

2 Tbsp. minced cilantro

2 Tbsp. finely chopped dill

Rib Eye Steaks

+ Eggplant Potato Salad
+ Tomato Salad

This steak is based on a recipe from chef Alain Ducasse. Halfway through cooking, the bone-in rib eyes are basted with a mixture of butter, thyme and garlic, so they're crusty outside and richly flavored. Grace Parisi's tomato salad side dish is a good choice for a hot summer night: It's quick, easy and full of flavor, combining sweet tomatoes with spicy horseradish and cooling buttermilk. The "not-your-everyday" potato salad combines smoky bacon and potatoes with silky eggplant. Dill and lemon add a bright, refreshing hit of flavor.

BUTTER-BASTED RIB EYE STEAKS

Active 25 min; Total 1 hr 10 min; Serves 4

Two 1¼-lb. bone-in rib eye steaks

Kosher salt and pepper

2 Tbsp. canola oil

4 Tbsp. unsalted butter

4 thyme sprigs

3 garlic cloves

1 rosemary sprig

1. Season the rib eye steaks all over with salt and pepper. Let the meat stand at room temperature for 30 minutes.

2. In a large cast-iron skillet, heat the canola oil until shimmering. Add the steaks and cook over high heat until crusty on the bottom, about 5 minutes. Turn the steaks and add the butter, thyme, garlic and rosemary to the skillet. Cook over high heat, basting the steaks with the melted butter, garlic and herbs, until medium-rare, 5 to 7 minutes longer. Transfer the steaks to a cutting board and let rest for 10 minutes. Cut the meat off the bone, then slice across the grain and serve. —*Alain Ducasse*

The Best Wine Pairings for Steak

CALIFORNIA AND WASHINGTON CABERNET BLENDS Napa Valley Cabernets with steak are a classic combo. For wines that are a little more interesting (and might be a better value), look for Cabernet blends (sometimes called Bordeaux-style blends) from lesser-known regions like California's Paso Robles and Washington state's Walla Walla.

BORDEAUX If you prefer European-style wines, red Bordeaux—which is made of a blend of Cabernet and Merlot, among other grapes—is a good bet. It tends to have more acid and tannins than the California wines, and you might appreciate that with a rich, buttery sauce. The somewhat savory flavors in Bordeaux can also be great with an herb-laden condiment. For affordable Bordeaux that is dominated by Cabernet, look for bottles from appellations like Haut-Médoc or Graves.

MALBEC Steak is to Argentineans what burgers are to Americans. In Argentina, you'll almost always find bottles of local Malbec on the table, and it's a great alternative to Cabernet. The rich, round, earthy reds (which many Americans now love) can sometimes even smell beefy. Yes, in this case, that's a good thing.

ZINFANDEL If you're rubbing your steak with sweet spices or brushing it with a dried chile sauce like mole, try berry-rich Zinfandel from California. This low-tannin red works well with some spice but is still rich enough to go with the steak. Zinfandel is also a good choice if you're serving barbecued meats like ribs.

TOMATO SALAD WITH HORSERADISH RANCH DRESSING

Total 20 min; Serves 4 to 6

¼ cup mayonnaise

¼ cup buttermilk

2 Tbsp. prepared horseradish

Flaky sea salt and pepper

2½ lbs. heirloom tomatoes and cherry tomatoes, chopped into different sizes

2 scallions, thinly sliced

In a small bowl, whisk the mayonnaise with the buttermilk and horseradish and season with salt and pepper. Arrange the tomatoes on plates and top with the scallions. Drizzle the dressing all around and serve right away. —*Grace Parisi*

EGGPLANT POTATO SALAD

Total 30 min; Serves 4

4 oz. thick-cut bacon, cut into lardons

2 Tbsp. extra-virgin olive oil

½ lb. baby red potatoes, quartered

1 small red onion, thinly sliced

2 Japanese eggplants (¾ lb.), quartered lengthwise and thinly sliced crosswise

Kosher salt and pepper

1 Tbsp. fresh lemon juice

2 Tbsp. chopped dill

In a large, deep skillet, cook the bacon over moderate heat, stirring, until lightly golden, about 5 minutes. Add the olive oil, potatoes, onion and eggplants and season with salt and pepper. Cover and cook over moderately low heat, stirring occasionally, until the eggplants and potatoes are tender and golden, 12 to 15 minutes. Stir in the lemon juice and dill and serve warm. —*Kay Chun*

Know Your Eggplants

ITALIAN The most recognizable type of eggplant, the Italian eggplant ranges from light purple to nearly black in color, with a thick skin. Typically 8 to 10 inches in size, Italian eggplants have a white flesh that develops great texture and flavor when cooked. They tend to soak up cooking liquid, so it's best to go light on oil, butter and cream.

WHITE White eggplants, as the name suggests, have a white skin. An heirloom variety of the Italian eggplant, they are smaller and sweeter than their purple counterparts.

JAPANESE Long and skinny, the Japanese eggplant can appear to be almost black in color. Unlike larger, tougher-skinned eggplants, which can require peeling, Japanese eggplants can be cooked and eaten with the skin on. They have a sweet taste and a creamy texture.

BABY Sometimes called Indian or patio eggplants, baby eggplants are tiny—about 2 to 3 inches in length, and do not require peeling. They range in color from white to green or purple, and from skinny to squat in shape. They have a mild, sweet flavor.

Grilled Lamb Chops
+ Corn on the Cob
+ Tomato-Feta Salad

This quintessential summer menu from chef April Bloomfield may just become your go-to menu of the season. Her trick for juicy lamb chops is to pound them so thin they cook in a flash, which keeps them moist on the grill. She also boils her corn in the husk to make removing the fine silk easier, then adds cheese and herb butter. And for the simple but spectacular salad, Bloomfield uses summer's best heirloom tomatoes and combines them with zippy garlic and lime.

THIN GRILLED LAMB CHOPS WITH LEMON
Total 30 min; Serves 4 to 6

12 lamb rib chops (2¼ lbs.), frenched (have your butcher do this)

Salt

Lemon wedges, for serving

1. On a work surface, wrap each lamb chop in 3 layers of plastic. Using a meat mallet or small saucepan, pound each chop to a ½-inch thickness.

2. Light a grill or preheat a grill pan over high heat. Season the lamb chops all over with salt. Grill over high heat until nicely charred on the bottom, about 2 minutes. Flip the chops and cook until medium rare within, 1 to 2 minutes longer. Transfer to a platter and serve with lemon wedges.
—April Bloomfield

CORN ON THE COB WITH PARSLEY BUTTER AND PARMESAN
Total 30 min; Serves 4 to 6

1 stick unsalted butter, softened

1 cup lightly packed parsley leaves

1 garlic clove, chopped

Kosher salt

4 to 6 ears of corn, in the husk

Maldon salt

Grated Parmigiano-Reggiano cheese, for sprinkling

Lemon wedges, for serving

1. Bring a pot of water to a boil. Meanwhile, in a food processor, pulse the butter with the parsley and garlic until the butter is whipped and the parsley is very finely chopped; scrape down the bowl as needed. Transfer the parsley butter to a small bowl and season with kosher salt.

2. Add the corn and a generous pinch of kosher salt to the boiling water and cook for 8 minutes. Using tongs, transfer the corn to a rack and let cool slightly.

3. Slice off the bottoms of the corn and slide off the husks. Generously brush the parsley butter all over the corn and sprinkle with Maldon salt and cheese. Serve with lemon wedges. —AB

MAKE AHEAD The parsley butter can be refrigerated overnight. Bring to room temperature before using.

TOMATO-FETA SALAD WITH LIME AND MINT

Total 20 min; Serves 4 to 6

5 to 6 large heirloom tomatoes (about 4 lbs.), each cut into 1-inch wedges

1 medium red onion, halved and thinly sliced

½ cup extra-virgin olive oil

1 Tbsp. finely grated lime zest, plus 6 Tbsp. fresh lime juice

1 garlic clove, minced

8 oz. feta cheese, crumbled

1 cup lightly packed mint leaves

Salt

Pepper

In a large bowl, toss the tomatoes with the onion, olive oil, lime zest, lime juice and garlic. Gently fold in the feta and mint. Season with salt and pepper and fold again. Serve right away. —*April Bloomfield*

+BONUS RECIPE: DESSERT

GRILLED FRUIT WITH HONEYED LEMON THYME VINEGAR

Total 30 min; Serves 6

2 Tbsp. extra-virgin olive oil, plus more for the grill

¼ cup honey

2 Tbsp. Lemon Thyme Vinegar (see Note)

2 medium peaches, cut into thick wedges

2 medium plums, halved

3 medium apricots, halved

2 medium nectarines, cut into thick wedges

Vanilla ice cream, for serving

1. Light a grill or heat a grill pan and brush lightly with oil. In a small saucepan, bring the honey and Lemon Thyme Vinegar to a simmer. Cook over very low heat for 5 minutes.

2. In a bowl, toss the fruit with the 2 tablespoons of oil. Grill the fruit over high heat, turning, until lightly charred in spots, about 3 minutes. Transfer to bowls, drizzle with the honeyed vinegar and serve with ice cream.
—*Dan Barber*

NOTE To make Lemon Thyme Vinegar, combine three 1-oz. bunches of lemon thyme, thick stems discarded, and 3 cups of Champagne vinegar in a 1-quart jar. Cover tightly and let stand at room temperature for 2 weeks. Discard the thyme sprigs.

Suggested Pairing

Serve the lamb chops with a herb-inflected, red-berried southern French red. Pair the tomato salad with a vibrant, medium-bodied Spanish Albariño.

Tomato-Feta Salad
with Lime and Mint

fall

Deviled Salmon   123
+Iceberg Wedges
+Squash Gratin

Baked Shrimp Risotto   127
+Roasted Tomatoes
+Grilled Fig Salad

Roasted Red Snapper   131
+Orzo Pilaf with Parsley
+Roasted Lemon Broccoli

Sautéed Chicken   134
+Torn Garlic Bread
+Heirloom Tomato Salad

Green Goddess Turkey Burgers   139
+Spicy Dill Quick Pickles
+Oven Fries

Lemon-Thyme Roast Chicken   143
+Classic Caesar Salad
+Wheat Berry Salad

Pork Schnitzel   147
+Cucumber Salad
+Fresh Cheese Spaetzle
+BONUS: DESSERT
  Cranberry Gingerbread

Rigatoni all'Amatriciana   151
+Black-Pepper Breadsticks
+Chicory-and-Beet Salad

Pork Meat Loaf   154
+Minty Peas and Carrots
+Mashed Potatoes

Tacos al Pastor   159
+Spicy Black Beans and Rice
+Chipotle-Roasted Carrots

Thyme-Basted Pork Tenderloin   163
+Roasted Acorn Squash
+Spicy Brussels Sprouts

Shaking Beef   166
+Edamame Fried Brown Rice
+Bok Choy with Mushrooms

Grilled Lamb   171
+Pickled Eggplant Salad
+Spiced Lentils
+BONUS: DESSERT
  Fallen Olive Oil Soufflé Cake

Deviled Salmon

+ Iceberg Wedges
+ Squash Gratin

Chef Eli Kulp uses four kinds of chiles—whole and in hot sauces—to make the spicy, sweet sauce for these salmon fillets. The sauce caramelizes as it cooks, so be sure to grill the fish over a not-too-hot fire to avoid charring. To balance the heat in the chile sauce, serve lettuce wedges topped with a roasted tomato dressing and a simple Gruyère squash gratin.

DEVILED SALMON
Active 30 min; Total 1 hr 30 min; Serves 4

1 ancho chile, stemmed and seeded

2 Tbsp. Sriracha

1 Tbsp. sambal oelek or other Asian chile-garlic sauce

1 Tbsp. extra-virgin olive oil

1 Tbsp. fresh lemon juice

2 garlic cloves, minced

1 hot pickled cherry pepper, stemmed, seeded and minced, plus 1 Tbsp. brine from the jar

Four 6-oz. skinless salmon fillets, about 1 inch thick

1. In a small bowl, cover the ancho chile with hot water and let stand until softened, about 20 minutes. Drain and mince the ancho. In a small bowl, whisk the ancho with all of the remaining ingredients except the salmon.

2. Add all but ¼ cup of marinade to a baking dish. Add salmon fillets and turn to coat. Cover and refrigerate salmon for at least 1 hour and up to 4 hours.

3. Light a grill. Grill the salmon fillets over moderate heat, turning once, until lightly charred and nearly cooked through, 6 to 8 minutes. Transfer the salmon to plates and serve with the reserved marinade. —*Eli Kulp*

4 More Ways to Prepare Salmon

MUSTARD-COATED Spread salmon fillets with a blend of Dijon mustard and dry mustard, then dip in mustard seeds and wheat germ to create a crisp crust in the skillet.

SPICE-RUBBED Try a mix of caraway and cumin seeds, ancho chile powder, garlic powder and salt. Be sure to toast and grind the seeds—it's worth the effort, as it adds so much flavor.

TERIYAKI Combine soy sauce, mirin or sweet sherry and sugar. Brush over salmon and broil or grill until the fish is done. Keep an eye on the salmon during cooking, though; the glaze can burn if the heat's too high.

WINE-POACHED Gently simmer salmon in a broth of white wine, water, herbs and aromatics. This classic cooking method gives the fish a delicate texture.

ICEBERG WEDGES WITH ROASTED TOMATO DRESSING

Active 30 min; Total 1 hr; Serves 4

½ lb. medium tomatoes, halved crosswise

⅓ cup extra-virgin olive oil, plus more for brushing

Kosher salt and pepper

2 Tbsp. sherry vinegar

1 Tbsp. fresh lemon juice

1 Tbsp. Dijon mustard

1 small shallot, quartered

1 small egg yolk

1 garlic clove

One 1-lb. head of iceberg lettuce, cut into 4 wedges through the core

¼ lb. baby carrots, preferably multicolored, thinly shaved lengthwise on a mandoline or with a vegetable peeler

4 radishes, very thinly sliced

Salted roasted pumpkin seeds and small dill sprigs, for garnish

1. Preheat the oven to 425°. On a rimmed baking sheet, brush the tomatoes with olive oil and season with salt and pepper. Roast the tomatoes for 20 to 25 minutes, until lightly browned in spots and softened. Let cool, then squeeze out and discard the seeds. Transfer the tomatoes to a blender. Add the sherry vinegar, lemon juice, mustard, shallot, egg yolk and garlic and puree until nearly smooth. With the blender on, gradually add the ⅓ cup of olive oil until incorporated. Season the dressing with salt and pepper.

2. Arrange the lettuce wedges on a platter. Scatter the carrot ribbons and sliced radishes over the lettuce and drizzle some of the dressing on top. Garnish with pumpkin seeds and dill sprigs and season the salad with salt and pepper. Serve right away, passing additional dressing at the table.

MAKE AHEAD The roasted tomato dressing can be refrigerated overnight.

Iceberg Wedges with Roasted Tomato Dressing

SQUASH GRATIN

Active 15 min; Total 45 min; Serves 4 to 6

2 Tbsp. extra-virgin olive oil, plus more for greasing

4 medium summer squash (zucchini and/or yellow squash), sliced lengthwise ⅛ inch thick

3 garlic cloves, sliced

Salt and pepper

1 cup panko (Japanese breadcrumbs)

3 oz. Gruyère cheese, shredded (1 cup)

Preheat the oven to 450°. Grease a 2-quart baking dish. In a large bowl, combine the squash, garlic and the 2 tablespoons of olive oil; season with salt and pepper and toss. Arrange the squash in the prepared dish and bake for 20 minutes, until tender. Sprinkle with the panko and cheese and bake for 10 minutes longer, until golden and crisp on top. —*Kay Chun*

Suggested Pairing

Pair the salmon with a citrusy Italian Vermentino.

Squash Gratin

Suggested Pairing

Serve the shrimp with a minerally Greek white such as Assyrtiko.

Baked Shrimp Risotto

+ Roasted Tomatoes
+ Grilled Fig Salad

In Kay Chun's "cheater's" risotto, there's no need to bother with stirring; instead, you bake the rice in the oven, then add shrimp and cheese at the very end. Serve with Grace Parisi's roasted tomatoes marinated with anchovies and capers. You can make the tomatoes ahead and store them, covered in olive oil, in the refrigerator, up to two weeks. Add grilled bread alongside the marinated tomatoes and a salad featuring fresh greens and a vibrant sesame, ginger and scallion dressing that brings together soft, sweet figs and crunchy nuts.

BAKED SHRIMP RISOTTO
Active 10 min; Total 30 min; Serves 4

2 Tbsp. extra-virgin olive oil

5 garlic cloves, sliced

1 cup arborio rice

3½ cups low-sodium chicken broth

½ cup freshly grated Parmigiano-Reggiano cheese, plus more for garnish

20 cooked shelled large shrimp

1 Tbsp. unsalted butter

1 Tbsp. fresh lemon juice

Kosher salt

Pesto sauce, for serving

Preheat the oven to 400°. In an enameled medium cast-iron casserole, heat the olive oil. Add the garlic and rice and cook over moderate heat, stirring, until very fragrant, 2 minutes. Stir in the broth and bring to a boil. Cover and bake for about 20 minutes, until the rice is tender. Stir in the ½ cup of cheese, the shrimp, butter and lemon juice; season with salt. Serve drizzled with pesto and garnished with cheese. —Kay Chun

How to Shell and Cook Raw Shrimp

1. Pull off the shrimp head and legs.

2. Using your thumbs, peel back and remove the shell.

3. Using a paring knife, make a shallow slit along the back of the shrimp.

4. Pull out the vein gently and discard.

5. To cook the shrimp, add the shelled and deveined shrimp to a large pot of salted boiling water and cook until the shrimp are pink and curled; the time will depend on the size of the shrimp (medium shrimp take only about 2 minutes). Drain and immediately cool under cold water to stop from further cooking.

ROASTED TOMATOES

Active 30 min; Total 4 hr; Serves 4

2 large shallots, sliced ¼ inch thick

¼ cup extra-virgin olive oil, plus more for marinating

5 lbs. plum tomatoes—peeled, halved and seeded

Salt and freshly ground pepper

One 2-oz. can anchovies, drained and finely chopped

¼ cup drained capers

1. Preheat the oven to 275˚. In a bowl, toss the shallots with 2 tablespoons of the olive oil and spread on a large, parchment paper-lined rimmed baking sheet. In the same bowl, toss the tomatoes with the remaining 2 tablespoons of olive oil and season with salt and pepper. Arrange the tomatoes over the shallots, cut sides up. Bake the tomatoes for 3 hours, until leathery but soft. Let cool.

2. In a large jar or glass bowl, layer the tomatoes and shallots with the anchovies and capers. Cover with olive oil and let stand for 30 minutes or refrigerate overnight. Serve with grilled bread. —*Grace Parisi*

GRILLED FIG SALAD WITH SPICED CASHEWS

Total 45 min; Serves 4 to 6

½ cup sugar

½ Tbsp. unsalted butter

¼ tsp. Chinese five-spice powder

1 cup raw cashews

Kosher salt

¼ cup canola oil, plus more for brushing

2 Tbsp. toasted sesame oil

2 Tbsp. unseasoned rice wine vinegar

3 Tbsp. finely grated peeled fresh ginger

3 scallions, green parts only, finely chopped (⅓ cup)

1 Tbsp. toasted black sesame seeds

12 fresh figs, halved

Pepper

2 heads of Bibb or oak leaf lettuce (10 oz.), leaves torn

1. Line a baking sheet with parchment paper. In a medium saucepan, bring the sugar and 2 tablespoons of water to a boil. Boil over moderately low heat, undisturbed, until a light amber caramel forms, about 5 minutes. Using a wet pastry brush, wash down any sugar crystals on the side of the pan. Remove from the heat and whisk in the butter and five-spice powder. Stir in the cashews until evenly coated. Scrape the cashews onto the prepared baking sheet and spread in an even layer; season with salt and cool. Break up the glazed cashews into individual pieces.

2. Meanwhile, in a small bowl, whisk the ¼ cup of canola oil with the sesame oil, rice wine vinegar, ginger, scallions and sesame seeds.

3. Light a grill and oil the grate. Brush the cut sides of the figs with oil and season with salt and pepper. Grill over moderate heat just until lightly charred and barely juicy, about 2 minutes per side; transfer to a plate.

4. In a large bowl, toss the lettuce with two-thirds of the dressing and season with salt and pepper. Arrange the lettuce on plates and top with the figs. Drizzle more dressing over the figs, sprinkle with the candied cashews and serve.

Roasted Red Snapper
+ Orzo Pilaf with Parsley
+ Roasted Lemon Broccoli

F&W's Justin Chapple brushes a whole red snapper with pimentón oil to give it a terrific smoky flavor, then roasts it packed in salt for moist, flaky flesh. It's served along with an herbed salad of tarragon and parsley. Melissa Rubel Jacobson's orzo pilaf is flavored simply with butter, onion and parsley. Tara Duggan's tangy lemon broccoli uses both the stalk and the florets to minimize waste and is paired with a rich tahini-yogurt dipping sauce.

PIMENTÓN-ROASTED RED SNAPPER WITH HERB SALAD
Active 40 min; Total 1 hr 15 min; Serves 4

¼ cup plus 1 Tbsp. extra-virgin olive oil

2 tsp. pimentón de la Vera (sweet smoked Spanish paprika)

1 tsp. finely grated lemon zest, plus ½ lemon, sliced

6 cups kosher salt (30 oz.), plus more for seasoning

3 large egg whites, beaten

One 2-lb. whole red snapper, cleaned

Ground black pepper

3 large bay leaves

5 medium celery ribs, thinly sliced on the diagonal

1 cup celery leaves

1 cup parsley leaves

½ cup tarragon leaves

2 Tbsp. fresh lemon juice

1. Preheat the oven to 425°. In a small bowl, whisk 3 tablespoons of the olive oil with the pimentón and lemon zest. In a large bowl, mix 6 cups of kosher salt with egg whites and ½ cup of water until it resembles moist sand.

2. Spread a ¼-inch-thick layer of the salt mixture in the center of a large rimmed baking sheet. Season the fish inside and out with black pepper and brush all over with the pimentón oil. Stuff the cavity with the lemon slices and bay leaves and lay the snapper on the salt. Mound the remaining salt mixture on top, lightly packing it to completely cover the fish.

3. Bake the fish for about 30 minutes, until an instant-read thermometer inserted into the fish through the salt registers 135°. Remove from the oven and let stand for 10 minutes. Crack the salt crust and discard it. Brush off any excess salt and transfer the fish to a platter.

4. In a large bowl, toss the celery with the celery leaves, parsley, tarragon, lemon juice and the remaining 2 tablespoons of olive oil. Season the salad with salt and pepper and serve alongside the fish. —*Justin Chapple*

How to Serve a Whole Fish

1. Using a serving spoon and fork, scrape away the small pin bones from the top and bottom of the fish where the fins connect to the body.

2. Following the natural division along the spine, split the top fillet in half with a serving fork or knife. Carefully lift off each piece of fillet.

3. Grasp the tail and lift to remove the bone cage and head. Scrape away any bones clinging to the fillets. Reassemble the fillets, drizzle with olive oil and serve.

ORZO PILAF WITH PARSLEY

Active 10 min; Total 30 min; Serves 4

3 Tbsp. unsalted butter

1 small onion, cut into ¼-inch dice

1 cup orzo

2 cups low-sodium chicken broth

Kosher salt and freshly ground pepper

Chopped flat-leaf parsley

In a large saucepan, melt the butter. Add the onion and cook over moderately high heat until tender, about 4 minutes. Add the orzo and cook, stirring frequently, until lightly toasted, about 3 minutes. Add the chicken broth and 1 teaspoon of salt and bring to a simmer. Cover and cook over low heat until the orzo is tender, about 18 minutes. Season with salt and pepper, fold in the parsley and serve. —*Melissa Rubel Jacobson*

ROASTED LEMON BROCCOLI WITH TAHINI-YOGURT SAUCE

Total 35 min; Serves 4

1½ lbs. broccoli—stalk trimmed and peeled, head cut into large florets

1 lemon, thinly sliced into ⅛-inch-thick rounds

3 Tbsp. extra-virgin olive oil

¼ tsp. crushed red pepper, plus more for garnish

Kosher salt

1 tsp. sesame seeds

½ cup plain Greek yogurt

2 Tbsp. tahini

1 Tbsp. fresh lemon juice

1 garlic clove, minced

Flaky sea salt, for garnish

1. Preheat the oven to 450°. Slice the broccoli stalk crosswise and the florets lengthwise ¼ inch thick; transfer to a rimmed baking sheet. Add the sliced lemon, olive oil and the ¼ teaspoon of crushed red pepper and season with kosher salt; toss to coat. Roast for about 10 minutes, until lightly browned. Stir in the sesame seeds and roast until the broccoli is tender, about 10 minutes longer.

2. Meanwhile, in a small bowl, whisk the yogurt with the tahini, lemon juice and garlic and season with kosher salt. Spread the yogurt sauce on a platter and top with the broccoli. Garnish with sea salt and crushed red pepper and serve warm. —*Tara Duggan*

MAKE AHEAD The tahini-yogurt sauce can be refrigerated for 2 days.

Suggested Pairing

Serve the snapper with a vibrant, herb-scented Loire Sauvignon Blanc.

Sautéed Chicken

\+ Torn Garlic Bread
\+ Heirloom Tomato Salad

This piquant dish from Lidia Bastianich with olives, capers and roasted lemons is one of our favorite ways to prepare skinless chicken breasts. Complete the menu with garlic bread and an heirloom tomato salad from Amelia O'Reilly and Nico Monday. The warm, garlicky anchovy dressing in the salad is fantastic with an assortment of juicy, late-season tomatoes.

Suggested Pairing

Serve the savory chicken with a light, crisp Rosato (an Italian rosé).

SAUTÉED CHICKEN WITH OLIVES, CAPERS AND ROASTED LEMONS

Total 35 min; Serves 4

¼ cup plus 2 Tbsp. extra-virgin olive oil, plus more for drizzling

2 lemons, sliced ¼ inch thick

Salt and pepper

Two 5-oz. bags baby spinach

2 Tbsp. plain dry breadcrumbs

Four 6-oz. boneless chicken breast halves

¼ cup all-purpose flour, for dusting

½ cup pitted green Sicilian or Spanish olives, sliced

2 Tbsp. drained capers

1 cup chicken stock or low-sodium broth

3 Tbsp. unsalted butter, cut into small dice

2 Tbsp. chopped flat-leaf parsley

1. Preheat the oven to 375°. Line a baking sheet with parchment paper. Drizzle olive oil on the parchment, then arrange the lemon slices in a single layer. Lightly drizzle the lemons with oil and season with salt and pepper. Roast for about 20 minutes, until the lemons begin to brown around the edges.

2. Meanwhile, heat a large, deep skillet. Add the spinach and cook over high heat, tossing, until wilted, about 2 minutes. Transfer the spinach to a strainer; press out the liquid. Wipe out the skillet and heat 2 tablespoons of the oil in it. Add the breadcrumbs and cook over moderate heat, stirring, until toasted, 2 minutes. Add the spinach, season with salt and pepper and cook for 1 minute.

3. In a medium, deep skillet, heat the remaining ¼ cup of oil. Season the chicken with salt and pepper and dust with the flour, shaking off the excess. Cook the chicken over high heat, turning once, until golden, about 6 minutes. Add the olives, capers and stock and bring to a boil. Cook over high heat until the stock is reduced by about two-thirds, about 5 minutes. Add the roasted lemons, butter and parsley, season with salt and pepper and simmer just until the chicken is cooked through, about 1 minute.

4. Transfer the chicken to plates and spoon the sauce on top. Serve the spinach on the side. —*Lidia Bastianich*

3 Ideas for Chicken Breasts from Powerhouse Chefs

PANKO-COATED
Thomas Keller of the French Laundry in Yountville, California, uses panko breadcrumbs to give chicken a crunchy crust. "Pounding chicken breasts to a uniform thickness cuts down on cooking time," he says.

SESAME CHICKEN SALAD Master chef Jean-Georges Vongerichten coats chicken breasts with sesame seeds, pan-roasts them until golden and juicy, then arranges them on a watercress and avocado salad drizzled with a gingery dressing.

BERBER-SPICED
Grilling guru Steven Raichlen rubs chicken breasts with a blend of North African spices that form a crispy crust on the grill. The result is full of what Raichlen calls "gutsy, in-your-face flavors."

TORN GARLIC BREAD

Active 10 min; Total 25 min; Serves 4

1 small shallot

1 garlic clove

½ stick unsalted butter, softened

Salt and pepper

10 oz. sourdough boule, torn into 2-inch pieces
(8 cups)

Chopped flat-leaf parsley, for garnish

1. Preheat the oven to 400°. In a mini food processor, pulse the shallot and garlic until finely chopped. Add the butter and puree until nearly smooth. Season the garlic butter with salt and pepper and scrape into a medium bowl.

2. Add the bread to the bowl and toss until coated. Spread the buttered bread on a large rimmed baking sheet and bake for 15 minutes, until crisp on the outside but chewy in the middle. Season with salt and pepper and transfer to a shallow bowl. Garnish with parsley and serve warm.
—*Amelia O'Reilly and Nico Monday*

Heirloom Tomato
Salad with Anchovy
Vinaigrette

HEIRLOOM TOMATO SALAD WITH ANCHOVY VINAIGRETTE

Total 30 min; Serves 4

¼ cup extra-virgin olive oil

4 anchovy fillets, minced

1 garlic clove, minced

1 tsp. finely grated lemon zest

1 medium shallot, thinly sliced

2 Tbsp. red wine vinegar

2 large eggs

1½ lbs. assorted heirloom tomatoes—large ones sliced, small ones halved

Fleur de sel and pepper

Flat-leaf parsley and marjoram leaves, for serving

1. In a small skillet, combine the olive oil, anchovies, garlic and lemon zest.

2. In a small bowl, toss the shallot with the vinegar and let stand for 10 minutes.

3. Bring a small saucepan of water to a boil. Turn the heat to low; when the water is simmering, gently place the eggs in the water. Cook for 6 minutes, until lightly boiled. Have an ice bath ready near the stove. With a slotted spoon, plunge the eggs in the ice bath and let cool for 2 minutes. Peel the eggs.

4. Arrange the tomatoes on plates and season with fleur de sel and pepper. Scatter the shallot and vinegar over the tomatoes.

5. Warm the anchovy dressing over moderate heat to a gentle simmer, then pour over the tomatoes. Cut the eggs in half crosswise and place a half on each plate. Scatter the parsley and marjoram over the salads and serve at once.
—*AO and NM*

Green Goddess Turkey Burgers
+ Spicy Dill Quick Pickles
+ Oven Fries

This tasty turkey burger from F&W's Justin Chapple gets its great flavor from anchovy, scallions and lots of fresh herbs mixed in with the ground turkey. And what's a burger without fries and some pickles? Grace Parisi's oven fries are flavored simply with salt, garlic, sage and rosemary and the easy pickles can be refrigerated either overnight or up to a month.

GREEN GODDESS TURKEY BURGERS
Total 30 min; Serves 4

½ lb. ground turkey

⅓ cup finely chopped basil

⅓ cup finely chopped scallions

⅓ cup finely chopped parsley

1 Tbsp. minced anchovy

Kosher salt and pepper

⅓ cup mayonnaise, plus more for serving

4 hamburger buns, split and toasted

Sliced red onion and baby greens, for serving

1. In a medium bowl, using a fork, gently stir the turkey with the basil, scallions, parsley, anchovy, 1 teaspoon of salt, ½ teaspoon of pepper and the ⅓ cup of mayonnaise. Using 2 round plastic lids from 1-quart take-out containers, press one-fourth of the turkey mixture into a perfect patty (see the illustration at right). Transfer to a plate. Repeat to form the remaining patties.

2. Light a grill or heat a grill pan. Season the patties lightly with salt and pepper and grill over moderately high heat, turning once, until cooked through, about 8 minutes. Transfer the burgers to the buns, top with mayonnaise, onion and greens and serve. —*Justin Chapple*

MAKE AHEAD The patties can be refrigerated for up to 3 hours before grilling.

How to Shape the Perfect Burger Patties

1. Take 2 lids from plastic takeout containers.

3. Invert the second lid on top and press down to flatten.

2. Mound 6 oz. of ground meat on the top of one lid.

4. Remove patty from the lids.

OVEN FRIES WITH HERBS AND PECORINO

Active 10 min; Total 1 hour; Serves 4

2 large baking potatoes, cut into 4-by-½-inch sticks

¼ cup extra-virgin olive oil

1 large garlic clove, minced

1 tsp. minced sage

1 tsp. minced rosemary

¼ cup freshly grated Pecorino Romano cheese

Kosher salt and freshly ground pepper

1. Preheat the oven to 425°. In a large bowl, toss the potato sticks with the olive oil until evenly coated. Spread the potato sticks on a rimmed baking sheet in a single layer and bake in the upper third of the oven, turning once or twice with a spatula, until they are golden and crispy, about 30 minutes.

2. Sprinkle the minced garlic and herbs over the fries and toss well. Roast for about 5 minutes longer, until the herbs are fragrant and the garlic is lightly browned. Transfer the fries to a large bowl and toss with the grated Pecorino Romano. Season with salt and pepper and serve. —GP

SPICY DILL QUICK PICKLES

Total 25 min plus overnight brining; Makes 2 quarts

12 oz. Kirby cucumbers, thinly sliced

12 oz. green beans, steamed 2 minutes and cooled

3 Tbsp. kosher salt

2 Tbsp. sugar

1¼ cups distilled white vinegar (5 percent acidity)

2 Tbsp. coriander seeds

6 large garlic cloves, halved

4 to 6 long red or green hot chiles, halved lengthwise

16 dill sprigs

1. Pack the vegetables into 2 clean 1-quart glass jars. In another jar, combine the salt, sugar, vinegar, coriander and garlic. Shake until the salt and sugar dissolve. Add 2 cups of water and pour the brine over the vegetables. Tuck the chiles and dill among the vegetables. Add enough water to keep the vegetables submerged. Close the jars and refrigerate overnight or for up to 1 month. —*Grace Parisi*

NOTE For each 1-quart jar, use 12 ounces of desired vegetables.

Suggested Pairing

Pair the turkey burgers with a fresh, full-flavored red such as one made from the versatile, food-friendly Barbera grape.

Suggested Pairing

Citrusy Sauvignon Blanc pairs nicely with the lemony chicken.

Lemon-Thyme Roast Chicken
+ Classic Caesar Salad
+ Wheat Berry Salad

Rubbing a simple lemon-and-butter mixture all over a whole chicken before roasting creates juicy, flavorful meat and crisp skin. Roasted chicken is a classic main dish in any season, but for a colorful and delicious autumn salad accompaniment, chef Stewart Dietz combines nutty-tasting einka wheat berries with kale and butternut squash. Any wheat berry will work well here, but larger varieties will take longer to cook. A traditional Caesar salad with romaine lettuce rounds out this perfect-for-fall meal.

LEMON-THYME ROAST CHICKEN
Active 15 min; Total 1 hr 15 min; Serves 4

½ stick plus 1 Tbsp. unsalted butter, softened

1½ Tbsp. thyme leaves

3 Tbsp. fresh lemon juice

Kosher salt and pepper

One 3½-lb. whole chicken, patted dry

1 lemon, quartered

1. Preheat the oven to 450°. In a small bowl, blend the ½ stick of butter with the thyme and 2 tablespoons of the lemon juice. Season with salt and pepper.

2. Season the chicken cavity with salt and pepper and tuck the lemon inside. Spread one-third of the lemon-thyme butter under the skin of the breasts and thighs. Rub the remaining butter all over the chicken and season with salt and pepper.

3. Set the chicken breast side up in a large cast-iron skillet. Roast for 40 to 45 minutes, until an instant-read thermometer inserted in the inner thigh registers 160°. Transfer the chicken to a carving board and let rest for 10 minutes.

4. Meanwhile, skim off all but 1 tablespoon of fat from the pan juices. Stir in the remaining 1 tablespoon of lemon juice and cook over moderate heat until hot, 1 to 2 minutes. Remove from the heat and stir in the remaining 1 tablespoon of butter. Season with salt and pepper.

5. Carve the chicken and transfer to a platter. Spoon the pan sauce on top and serve.

3 Ways to Tell When Roast Chicken Is Done

THERMOMETER
The most foolproof way to know when a chicken is done is to insert a well-calibrated instant-read thermometer into the meat near the inner thigh (between the leg and the breast, but make sure you're not hitting bone). If the thermometer reads between 160° and 165°, it's done. If the temperature is lower, it needs more time in the oven; much higher, and it's overcooked. Don't panic—just use the pan's juices to help moisten any dry meat.

THE JUICES RUN CLEAR Slice the skin between the leg and the breast and peek at the juices. If they're clear, the chicken is likely done. If they're slightly pink, try the next test.

THE MEAT IS FIRM
When the chicken is cooked, the meat should feel firm instead of jiggly or rubbery. And it shouldn't be tight (a sign of overcooking). When you're checking the juices near the inner thigh, check the meat. If it's undercooked, continue to roast. Or cut off the legs and throw them back in the oven while you carve the breast.

CLASSIC CAESAR SALAD

Total 30 min; Serves 6 to 8

½ lb. baguette, cut into 1-inch cubes

½ cup plus 2 Tbsp. extra-virgin olive oil

Salt

1 large egg yolk

4 oil-packed anchovy fillets, drained

2 garlic cloves, chopped

2 Tbsp. red wine vinegar

2 Tbsp. fresh lemon juice

⅛ tsp. cayenne pepper

1½ lbs. romaine lettuce, torn into bite-size pieces

½ cup freshly grated Parmigiano-Reggiano cheese (about 1½ oz.)

1. Preheat the oven to 375°. On a large rimmed baking sheet, toss the bread cubes with 2 tablespoons of the olive oil; spread in an even layer and season with salt. Bake the baguette cubes for about 15 minutes, until golden.
—*Brian Perrone*

2. Meanwhile, in a blender, combine the egg yolk, anchovy fillets, garlic, vinegar, lemon juice and cayenne and puree. With the machine on, slowly add the remaining ½ cup of olive oil and blend until incorporated. Season with salt.

3. In a large bowl, toss the romaine with the croutons, dressing and cheese and serve. —*Brian Perrone*

WHEAT BERRY SALAD WITH TUSCAN KALE AND BUTTERNUT SQUASH

Active 20 min; Total 50 min; Serves 4 to 6

1 lb. peeled butternut squash, cut into ½-inch dice (3 cups)

6 Tbsp. extra-virgin olive oil

Salt and freshly ground pepper

2 cups whole einka or other wheat berries

10 oz. Tuscan kale, stemmed, leaves sliced crosswise ¼ inch thick (4 cups)

2 Tbsp. sherry vinegar

½ cup minced shallots

1 Tbsp. finely chopped sage

2 garlic cloves, minced

⅝ cup dry white wine

¼ cup chopped flat-leaf parsley

1. Preheat the oven to 400°. On a rimmed baking sheet, toss the squash with 2 tablespoons of the olive oil and season with salt and pepper. Roast the squash for 20 to 25 minutes, until tender. Transfer to a large bowl.

2. In a medium saucepan, cover the wheat berries with 5 cups of water and ¼ teaspoon of salt and bring to a boil. Simmer over moderate heat until tender, 25 minutes.

3. Add the kale to the wheat berries, cover and remove from the heat; let stand until the kale is wilted, 5 minutes. Drain well and add the wheat and kale to the squash. Add the vinegar and 2 tablespoons of the oil to the salad, season with salt and pepper and toss.

4. In a medium skillet, heat remaining 2 tablespoons of oil. Add shallots and a pinch of salt and cook over moderately high heat until just starting to brown, 3 to 4 minutes. Add sage and cook for 1 minute, until fragrant. Add garlic and cook, stirring, for 1 minute. Add wine and simmer until evaporated. Add shallot and garlic to salad and toss. Season with salt and pepper and garnish with parsley.
—*Stewart Dietz*

Pork Schnitzel

+ Cucumber Salad
+ Fresh Cheese Spaetzle

It takes only five minutes to cook pork cutlets into perfect schnitzel. With only a handful of ingredients, a crisp and bright salad of cucumbers with dill and yogurt is a simple accompaniment to the meal. For the spaetzle side dish, Grace Parisi uses small-curd cottage cheese in the spaetzle and makes the chive sauce with tangy quark. Adding 2 tablespoons of granulated sugar instead of the chives turns this savory dish into a delicious dessert.

PORK SCHNITZEL
WITH CUCUMBER SALAD

Total 45 min; Serves 4

6 Persian cucumbers, sliced ½ inch thick

Kosher salt and pepper

¼ cup finely chopped dill, plus small sprigs for garnish

1¾ cups whole-milk yogurt

1½ cups seasoned breadcrumbs

One 1¼-lb. pork tenderloin, cut on the bias into 12 thin slices, about ¼ inch thick

Canola oil, for frying

1. In a colander, toss the cucumbers with 1 teaspoon of salt. Let stand for 15 minutes, then gently squeeze out the excess water. In a large bowl, mix the cucumbers with the chopped dill and ¼ cup of the yogurt and season with salt and pepper.

2. Meanwhile, put the breadcrumbs and the remaining 1½ cups of yogurt in 2 separate shallow bowls. Season the pork with salt and pepper and dip in the yogurt, letting the excess drip back into the bowl. Dredge in the breadcrumbs, pressing to flatten the pork and help the crumbs adhere.

3. In a large skillet, heat ¼ inch of oil until shimmering. In batches, add the pork in a single layer and cook over moderately high heat, turning once, until browned and crispy, about 5 minutes. Transfer to paper towels to drain. Serve the pork with the cucumber salad and garnish with small sprigs of dill. —*Justin Chapple*

Chef Upgrades
for Pork Tenderloin

ENHANCE WITH BOLD INGREDIENTS
San Francisco chef Adam Sobel fills soft tortillas with grilled tenderloin and tart, spicy toppings like grilled pineapple, charred jalapeño, pickled red onion and fresh cilantro.

PREPARE WITH TANGY DAIRY
By soaking the tenderloin in acidic dairy like buttermilk, yogurt or sour cream before cooking, Chicago chef Jason Vincent adds rich flavor while tenderizing the meat.

RUB WITH ANCHOVY PASTE
John Stewart, co-chef of Zazu in Sonoma County, California, seasons tenderloin with briny flavors, like an anchovy paste mixed with garlic and olive oil. The end result isn't fishy, just complex.

TOP WITH LUSCIOUS CONDIMENTS
Scott Romano of Frisco Gun Club in Dallas slices tenderloin thin, piles it in a sandwich and spreads on strong, rich condiments, such as herbed aioli.

CREATE THE ILLUSION OF FAT WITH BEANS
Duskie Estes, also co-chef of Zazu in Sonoma County, likes to mimic the silky texture of pork fat by serving tenderloin with creamy white gigante beans cooked with caramelized onions, lime juice and cilantro.

FRESH CHEESE SPAETZLE
Total 25 min; Serves 4

2 large eggs, lightly beaten

¼ cup plus 1 Tbsp. milk

¼ cup small-curd cottage cheese (see Note)

Kosher salt and freshly ground pepper

1 cup all-purpose flour

2 Tbsp. unsalted butter

½ cup quark (see Note)

1½ Tbsp. snipped chives

1. Bring a large pot of salted water to a boil. In a medium bowl, beat the eggs with the milk, cottage cheese, ½ teaspoon of salt and ¼ teaspoon of pepper. Stir in the flour until a smooth, thick, sticky batter forms.

2. Spoon the batter into a colander with ¼-inch holes. Set or hold the colander 1 inch above the boiling water and, using a rubber spatula, scrape the batter through the holes. Stir the spaetzle once or twice to separate them. As soon as they rise to the surface, use a slotted spoon to transfer them to a clean colander; drain well.

3. Melt the butter in a large nonstick skillet. Add the boiled spaetzle and cook over moderately high heat, stirring and shaking the skillet occasionally, until the spaetzle are browned and crisp in spots, about 5 minutes. Add the quark and snipped chives, reduce the heat to moderately low and cook, stirring, until the sauce is creamy, 1 to 2 minutes. Season the spaetzle with salt and pepper and serve right away. —*Grace Parisi*

NOTE You can substitute farmer cheese for the cottage cheese. In place of the quark, feel free to use crème fraîche, fromage blanc, lebneh or mascarpone.

MAKE AHEAD The boiled cheese spaetzle can be covered in plastic wrap and kept at room temperature for up to 2 hours before sautéing.

+BONUS RECIPE: DESSERT
CRANBERRY GINGERBREAD
Active 20 min; Total 1 hr 20 min plus cooling; Serves 8

½ cup canola oil, plus more for greasing

¾ cup unsulfured molasses

¾ cup packed light brown sugar

2 large eggs

1 Tbsp. finely grated peeled fresh ginger

1½ cups fresh cranberries (6 oz.), coarsely chopped

2 cups all-purpose flour

2 tsp. baking powder

½ tsp. baking soda

½ tsp. ground cinnamon

½ tsp. ground cloves

¼ tsp. kosher salt

1. Preheat the oven to 350°. Grease an 8-by-4-inch loaf pan. In a large bowl, whisk the ½ cup of canola oil with the molasses, brown sugar, eggs, ginger and cranberries. In a medium bowl, sift the flour with the baking powder, baking soda, cinnamon, cloves and salt. Whisk the flour mixture into the molasses mixture until well blended.

2. Scrape the batter into the prepared pan and bake for about 50 minutes, until a cake tester inserted in the center comes out clean with a few moist crumbs attached. Transfer to a rack and let cool for 10 minutes, then unmold the gingerbread and let cool to room temperature before slicing and serving. —*Kay Chun*

MAKE AHEAD The gingerbread can be stored in an airtight container at room temperature for up to 3 days.

Suggested Pairing

Serve the pork schnitzel with an aromatic, fruit forward Pinot Noir from New Zealand.

Fresh Cheese Spaetzle

Rigatoni all'Amatriciana
+ Black-Pepper Breadsticks
+ Chicory-and-Beet Salad

This weeknight pasta dish from Mario Batali is spicy and porky with plenty of rich tomato flavor. To simplify dinner preparations, you can make the sauce the day before and reheat gently before tossing with the pasta. Salad and breadsticks are the perfect partners for the pasta. Chef Naomi Pomeroy recommends soaking bitter greens like radicchio and escarole in ice water before serving them in salads to eliminate some of the bitterness and make them extra crisp. Serve Scott Conant's peppery breadsticks with balsamic-drizzled cheese.

RIGATONI ALL'AMATRICIANA
Total 30 min; Serves 6 to 8

1 lb. rigatoni

¼ cup extra-virgin olive oil

¼ lb. thick-cut bacon, sliced crosswise ¼ inch wide

1 medium red onion, halved and thinly sliced

¼ cup tomato paste

2 tsp. crushed red pepper

1¼ cups strained tomatoes

½ cup freshly grated pecorino cheese, plus more for serving

½ cup chopped parsley, plus more for garnish

Kosher salt and black pepper

1. In a large saucepan, cook the rigatoni until al dente. Drain the pasta, reserving 1 cup of the cooking water.

2. Meanwhile, in another large saucepan, heat the olive oil. Add the bacon and onion and cook over moderately high heat, stirring occasionally, until the onion is softened and the bacon is browned, 5 to 7 minutes. Add the tomato paste and crushed red pepper and cook, stirring, for 1 minute. Stir in the strained tomatoes and bring the sauce just to a simmer.

3. Add the pasta and reserved cooking water to the sauce and cook over moderate heat, tossing, until the pasta is coated. Remove from the heat and stir in the ½ cup each of cheese and parsley. Season the pasta with salt and black pepper and transfer to bowls. Garnish with chopped parsley and serve, passing more cheese at the table.
—Mario Batali

Pairing Pasta Shapes and Sauces

PENNE RIGATE is a small, ribbed, tube-shaped pasta cut on the diagonal. It works well in smooth sauces, chunky ragùs and pasta salads.

BUCATINI is a long, hollow strand that's perfect for soaking up tomato-based sauces.

STROZZAPRETI ("priest strangler") has a delicate twisted shape that's great for catching olive oil and thinner sauces like pesto and marinara.

FUSILLI LUNGHI BUCATI is a long, hollow, coiled pasta that's sturdy enough to hold Bolognese or thick cream sauces.

BLACK-PEPPER BREADSTICKS
Active 30 min; Total 2 hr; Makes 32 breadsticks

1 cup warm water

1 Tbsp. active dry yeast (about 1½ envelopes)

3 cups plus 2 Tbsp. bread flour

¾ cup solid vegetable shortening

4 tsp. kosher or Maldon salt

1½ tsp. freshly ground black pepper

1. Preheat the oven to 350°. Line 3 baking sheets with parchment paper. In the bowl of a stand mixer fitted with the dough hook, combine the water, yeast and 2 tablespoons of the flour and let stand until foamy, about 5 minutes. Add the remaining 3 cups of flour along with the shortening, salt and pepper and knead at medium speed until the dough is smooth and elastic, 7 to 8 minutes. Cover the bowl with plastic wrap and let the dough rest for 15 minutes.

2. Turn dough out onto an unfloured surface; divide into fourths. Cut each quarter into 8 pieces. Roll each piece into a 9-by-½-inch rope. Using a knife, trim breadsticks to 8 inches; arrange on baking sheets and bake for 45 minutes, until golden and firm, shifting pans halfway through baking. Transfer breadsticks to racks; let cool. —*Scott Conant*

CHICORY-AND-BEET SALAD WITH PINE NUT VINAIGRETTE
Total 45 min; Serves 6

1 small head of escarole, white and light green leaves only, torn

½ head of radicchio, cored and torn into bite-sized pieces

1 Belgian endive, halved lengthwise, cored and cut into bite-size pieces

3 Tbsp. pine nuts

3 Tbsp. extra-virgin olive oil

3 Tbsp. sherry vinegar

2 small garlic cloves, finely grated

1½ tsp. honey

Kosher salt and pepper

4 baby golden or Chioggia beets, scrubbed and very thinly sliced

1 medium fennel bulb—halved lengthwise, cored and very thinly sliced, fennel fronds chopped

1. Set up a large ice water bath. Add the escarole, radicchio and endive to the ice bath and let stand for 30 minutes.

2. Meanwhile, in a small skillet, toast the pine nuts over moderate heat until golden and fragrant, about 5 minutes. Let cool; transfer to a food processor. Add the oil, vinegar, garlic and honey, season with salt and pepper and puree until smooth.

3. Drain the greens and spin or pat dry. Transfer to a large chilled bowl, add the beets and sliced fennel and toss well. Drizzle half of the dressing around the side of the bowl, season with salt and pepper and toss. Drizzle with the remaining dressing and toss again. Top with the fennel fronds and serve right away. —*Naomi Pomeroy*

Suggested Pairing

Pair the pasta with an herb-scented, dark-berried Italian red.

Pork Meat Loaf
+ Minty Peas and Carrots
+ Mashed Potatoes

The pork meat loaf is inspired by chef Andrew Carmellini's recipe for juicy pork loin meatballs braised in a spicy tomato-chickpea sauce. For this easier version, mix the meat in a food processor, shape the meat into a loaf, and cook in a spicy tomato sauce blended with prepared hummus. Grace Parisi's mashed potatoes and minty peas from Melissa Rubel Jacobson are classic sides for meat loaf.

PORK MEAT LOAF WITH HUMMUS

Active 25 min; Total 1 hr 10 min; Serves 4

Two 1-inch-thick slices of Italian bread, crusts removed, bread soaked in 1 cup of milk and squeezed dry

2 oz. sliced bacon

2 oz. sliced prosciutto

1 small onion, thinly sliced

1 garlic clove, very finely chopped

2 oil-packed sun-dried tomatoes

½ roasted red pepper from a jar

1 large egg

1 Tbsp. chopped flat-leaf parsley

½ tsp. chopped thyme

½ tsp. crushed red pepper

¼ tsp. dried oregano

Kosher salt and black pepper

1¼ lbs. lean ground pork

1½ tsp. extra-virgin olive oil, plus more for brushing

½ cup tomato puree

½ cup chicken stock or low-sodium broth

¼ cup prepared plain hummus

1. In a food processor, pulse the bread, bacon and prosciutto. Add the onion, garlic, sun-dried tomatoes, roasted pepper and egg; process to a paste. Pulse in the parsley, thyme, crushed red pepper, oregano and ½ teaspoon each of salt and pepper. Transfer to a large bowl and knead in the pork.

2. Preheat the broiler. Pat the mixture into one 8-inch-long loaf. In a large nonstick roasting pan, heat the 1½ teaspoons of oil. Place the loaf in the pan and cook over moderate heat until the bottom is browned, 6 minutes. Brush the top with oil, transfer to the broiler and broil until slightly browned. Turn the oven to 350°.

3. In a small bowl, combine the tomato puree, stock and hummus. Pour the mixture into the roasting pan and bake for 30 minutes, or until an instant-read thermometer inserted into the center of the loaf registers 180°.

4. Turn on the broiler. Spoon some of the sauce over the loaf and broil until browned. Transfer to a platter and serve with the gravy. —Andrew Carmellini

MINTY PEAS AND CARROTS

Total 15 min; Serves 4

1 Tbsp. extra-virgin olive oil

3 carrots, cut into ½-inch dice

1 large shallot, halved and thinly sliced

¾ lb. frozen baby peas, thawed

1 Tbsp. thinly sliced mint leaves

1 Tbsp. unsalted butter

Kosher salt and black pepper

In a medium skillet, heat the oil. Add the carrots and shallot and cook over moderate heat, stirring frequently, until the carrots are just tender, about 8 minutes. Add the peas and cook, stirring, until heated through, about 5 minutes. Remove from the heat and stir in the mint and butter. Season with salt and pepper and serve.
—Melissa Rubel Jacobson

Suggested Pairing

Serve the meat loaf with a robust, earthy Aglianico from southern Italy.

MASHED POTATOES
WITH CRISPY SHALLOTS
Total 45 min; Serves 4 to 6

3 lbs. Yukon Gold potatoes, peeled and quartered
(see Note)

2 garlic cloves, peeled

1 cup canola oil

3 large shallots, thinly sliced (1½ cups)

½ cup half-and-half

6 Tbsp. unsalted butter

Kosher salt

1. In a large pot, cover the potatoes and garlic cloves with cold water and bring to a boil. Simmer over moderate heat until the potatoes are tender when pierced with a fork, about 20 minutes.

2. Meanwhile, in a medium skillet, heat the canola oil until shimmering. Add the shallots in a single layer and cook over moderate heat, stirring frequently, until they are golden, about 15 minutes. Using a slotted spoon, transfer the shallots to paper towels to drain.

3. Drain the potatoes and garlic in a colander, shaking out the excess water. Add the half-and-half and butter to pot and heat until melted. Remove from the heat. Press the potatoes and garlic through a ricer into the pot and season with salt. Stir and cook over moderate heat until very hot. Transfer the mashed potatoes to a bowl. Just before serving, sprinkle the shallots with salt and garnish the potatoes with the fried shallots. —*Grace Parisi*

NOTE Yukon Golds have a naturally creamy texture, which makes them ideal for mashed potatoes.

MAKE AHEAD The mashed potatoes can be made earlier in the day and kept at room temperature; warm over moderate heat, stirring constantly. The fried shallots can be kept in an airtight container for up to 3 days; reheat in the oven if desired.

Potato Primer

STARCHY Potatoes like russets are relatively dry and starchy. They tend to disintegrate in soups and stews but are perfect for mashing, baking and French frying.

WAXY Low-starch, waxy potatoes include Red Bliss, fingerlings and new potatoes (any young potato whose sugars haven't fully converted to starch). They have moist flesh that remains firm during cooking, so they're ideal for roasts, stews, casseroles and potato salads.

ALL-PURPOSE Potatoes with medium starch and moisture levels— Yukon Golds, Adirondack Blues and purple potatoes, to name a few—generally hold up better to long cooking than starchy potatoes. They can be boiled, roasted or pan-fried and also make fabulous mashed potatoes and gratins.

Tacos al Pastor
+ Spicy Black Beans and Rice
+ Chipotle-Roasted Carrots

Chef Courtney Contos' smart hack of the classic Mexican recipe gives you all the flavor without all the fuss. Rather than marinating the pork shoulder for days, and then spit-roasting, you marinate it overnight, then grill for less than five minutes. Phoebe Lapine's spicy black beans get their kick from a mix of hot sauce and chili powder and Alex Stupak's carrots are roasted simply with smoky canned chipotles in adobo, then served with peppery watercress, sesame seeds and cooling yogurt.

TACOS AL PASTOR
Total 1 hr plus overnight marinating; Serves 8

1 Tbsp. canola oil, plus more for brushing

3 garlic cloves

1 tsp. dried oregano

½ tsp. ground cumin

½ tsp. pepper

¼ tsp. ground cloves

4 guajillo chiles—stemmed, seeded and cut into 2-inch pieces

⅓ cup pineapple juice

¼ cup distilled white vinegar

2 Tbsp. achiote paste

Sea salt

2 lbs. boneless pork shoulder, sliced ¼ inch thick

½ medium pineapple, peeled and sliced ½ inch thick

1 medium red onion, sliced crosswise ½ inch thick

Warm corn tortillas, chopped cilantro and lime wedges, for serving

1. In a medium saucepan, heat the 1 tablespoon of oil. Add the garlic and cook over moderately high heat, turning occasionally, until lightly browned, about 1 minute. Stir in the oregano, cumin, pepper and cloves and cook until fragrant, about 1 minute. Add the chiles and cook, stirring, until blistered in spots, about 30 seconds. Add the pineapple juice, vinegar and achiote paste and bring to a boil. Remove from the heat and let stand for 5 minutes.

2. Transfer the chile mixture to a blender and puree until smooth. Season with salt. Scrape the marinade into a large, sturdy plastic bag. Add the pork and turn to coat. Set the bag in a small baking dish and refrigerate overnight.

3. Light a grill or heat a grill pan. Brush the pineapple and onion with oil and grill over high heat, turning once, until lightly charred and softened, 3 to 5 minutes. Transfer to a carving board and tent with foil.

4. Remove pork from marinade and grill over high heat until pork is lightly charred and just cooked through, about 2 to 4 minutes. Transfer to carving board and let rest for 5 minutes.

5. Cut the pineapple, onion and pork into thin strips and transfer to a bowl. Season with salt. Serve with corn tortillas, chopped cilantro and lime wedges.

—*Courtney Contos*

3 Tips from Taco Expert Aarón Sánchez

DOUBLE STACK Sánchez opts for 4-inch corn tortillas, double-stacked, to maintain the taco's integrity. If you have a 6-inch tortilla and take a bite, things start falling out.

The 4-inch tortillas keep everything compact.

GET THE MEAT PLACEMENT RIGHT Keep a quarter-inch border of tortilla around the taco so the contents won't spill out.

ADD PICKLES Sánchez uses the bright flavor of something pickled to cut through the richness of the meat.

SPICY BLACK BEANS AND RICE

Active 10 min; Total 35 min; Serves 8

2 cups white basmati rice

3½ cups water

Two 15-oz. cans black beans, rinsed and drained

2 Tbsp. Worcestershire sauce

2 tsp. hot sauce

1 tsp. cumin

1 tsp. chili powder

1 tsp. sea salt

2 cups chicken stock, vegetable stock or water

2 Tbsp. fresh lime juice

Cilantro leaves, for garnish

1. In a large saucepan, cover the rice with the water. Bring to a simmer, cover and cook over low heat until the rice is tender and the water has been absorbed, about 18 minutes. Remove the saucepan from the heat and let stand, covered, for 5 minutes.

2. Meanwhile, in another large saucepan, combine the beans, Worcestershire, hot sauce, cumin, chili powder, salt and stock or water. Bring to a simmer, then turn the heat down to medium-low and cook, stirring occasionally, until the beans are tender and the liquid has thickened, about 25 minutes. Stir in the lime juice and taste for seasoning.

3. Transfer the rice to a platter. Top with the beans and garnish with cilantro. —*Phoebe Lapine*

CHIPOTLE-ROASTED BABY CARROTS

Active 20 min; Total 1 hr; Serves 8

40 thin baby carrots (3 to 4 bunches) carrots scrubbed and keeping tops

2 chipotle chiles in adobo, minced, plus 1 tsp. of adobo sauce from the can

1 Tbsp. unsulfured molasses

3½ Tbsp. extra-virgin olive oil

Salt and pepper

¼ cup sesame seeds

5 oz. watercress, thick stems discarded

Greek yogurt, for serving

1. Preheat the oven to 350°. Toss the carrots on a rimmed baking sheet with the chipotles, molasses and 3 tablespoons of the olive oil; season with salt and pepper. Roast for 30 to 35 minutes, until the carrots are crisp-tender and browned. Transfer the carrots to a plate and let them cool completely.

2. Meanwhile, in a small skillet, toast the sesame seeds over moderate heat, tossing, until golden, 3 to 5 minutes. Stir in the remaining ½ tablespoon of olive oil and season with salt; let cool.

3. On the plate, toss the carrots with the 1 teaspoon of adobo sauce. Arrange the carrots on plates and scatter the watercress on top. Garnish with the sesame seeds and serve with yogurt. —*Alex Stupak*

MAKE AHEAD The roasted carrots can be kept at room temperature for up to 4 hours.

Suggested Pairing

Have these tasty tacos with a crisp, lightly malty beer, like an amber ale, or a robust, dark-fruited red, such as an Argentinean Malbec.

Thyme-Basted Pork Tenderloin
+ Roasted Acorn Squash
+ Spicy Brussels Sprouts

This easy Parisian entrée from chef Dai Shinozuka combines juicy pan-roasted pork tenderloin, meaty mushrooms and an enticing, crunchy topping of walnuts, shallots and chives. To accompany the pork tenderloin, make the most of fall produce and serve a brown sugar-roasted acorn squash from Todd Porter and Diane Cu and spicy Brussels sprouts from Joanne Chang. The staff at Boston's Myers + Chang restaurant call these Brussels sprouts "green candy" because they get so sweet as they brown in the skillet.

THYME-BASTED PORK TENDERLOIN WITH OYSTER MUSHROOMS

Total 45 min; Serves 4

1 Tbsp. grapeseed oil

One 1¼-lb. pork tenderloin

Kosher salt and pepper

4 Tbsp. unsalted butter

¼ cup extra-virgin olive oil

1½ lbs. oyster mushrooms, trimmed and torn into 1-inch pieces

4 garlic cloves, 2 minced and 2 crushed

2 Tbsp. chopped parsley

2 large thyme sprigs

Toasted walnuts, chopped shallot and chives and flaky sea salt, for garnish

1. Preheat oven to 425°. In a 12-inch ovenproof skillet, heat the grapeseed oil until shimmering. Season the pork with salt and pepper and cook over moderately high heat until browned all over, about 5 minutes. Transfer to the oven and roast the pork until an instant-read thermometer inserted in the thickest part registers 135°, 18 to 20 minutes.

2. Meanwhile, in a very large skillet, melt 1 tablespoon of the butter in the olive oil. Add mushrooms, season with salt and pepper and cook over moderately high heat, turning occasionally, until golden, about 15 minutes. Add the minced garlic and parsley and cook, stirring, until garlic is fragrant, about 30 seconds. Remove from heat.

3. Set the pork over moderate heat. Add the remaining 3 tablespoons of butter, the crushed garlic and the thyme to the skillet and cook until the butter is foamy. Baste the meat with the butter just until the butter browns, 2 to 3 minutes.

4. Transfer the pork to a cutting board and cut into thick slices. Spoon the mushrooms onto a platter, top with the pork and drizzle with the brown butter. Garnish with walnuts, shallot, chives and flaky salt and serve.
—*Dai Shinozuka*

Know Your Pork Cuts: Loin and Tenderloin

Pork loin and pork tenderloin are not interchangeable in recipes.

PORK LOIN is much larger than the tenderloin—a whole loin can be almost three feet long. This cut is usually butchered and sold as ribs, chops and roasts.

PORK TENDERLOIN is a long, thin cylinder of boneless meat that sits just below the loin. It's naturally lean, mild in flavor and the most tender cut of pork, when cooked quickly.

SPICY-AND-GARLICKY BRUSSELS SPROUTS

Total 30 min; Serves 4 to 6

1½ lbs. Brussels sprouts, halved

3 Tbsp. vegetable oil

2 large garlic cloves, smashed

½ tsp. crushed red pepper

Kosher salt

1. Bring a large pot of salted water to a boil. Add the Brussels sprouts and cook until bright green, about 2 minutes. Drain well and pat dry.

2. In a large, deep skillet, heat the oil until shimmering. Add the garlic and Brussels sprouts and cook over high heat undisturbed for 1 minute. Add the crushed red pepper, season with salt and cook over moderate heat, stirring a few times, until the Brussels sprouts are browned and tender, about 3 minutes. Transfer to a bowl and serve warm. —*Joanne Chang*

CLASSIC BROWN SUGAR-ROASTED ACORN SQUASH

Active 10 min; Total 1 hr; Serves 4

1 stick unsalted butter, melted

2 Tbsp. brown sugar

2 medium acorn squash (about 2 lbs. each), halved and seeded

Kosher or sea salt and freshly cracked black pepper

1. Preheat the oven to 400°. Line a baking sheet with parchment paper. In a small bowl, combine the butter and sugar. Brush the cut sides of the squash halves with the brown sugar butter and season with salt and pepper.

2. Set the squash halves cut side down on the prepared baking sheet and roast for 30 minutes. Turn the squash cut side up and brush with juices from the pan. Continue roasting for about 20 minutes, or until tender, then serve. —*Todd Porter and Diane Cu*

Suggested Wine Pairing

Serve the pork tenderloin with an herb-scented, medium-bodied Cabernet Franc.

Shaking Beef
+ Edamame Fried Brown Rice
+ Bok Choy with Mushrooms

Cubes of beef tenderloin are super tender in this wonderfully spiced and elegant Vietnamese classic from Marcia Kiesel. It's called "shaking beef" because you shake the pan to toss the beef while cooking it. Edamame is a great addition to the simple fried brown rice from Todd Porter and Diane Cu, and Bryant Ng's bok choy is char-grilled until smoky and topped with braised shiitake and oyster sauce.

SHAKING BEEF

Active 30 min; Total 1 hr 30 min; Serves 4

1 lb. filet mignon, cut into 1-inch pieces

3½ Tbsp. sugar

⅓ cup plus 1 Tbsp. canola oil

Kosher salt and freshly ground pepper

3 Tbsp. light soy sauce

3 Tbsp. Asian fish sauce

2 Tbsp. white vinegar

1 tsp. rice wine (optional)

6 scallions, cut into 1-inch pieces

1 small red onion, thinly sliced

3 garlic cloves, minced

1 Tbsp. unsalted butter

Watercress and lime wedges, for serving

1. In a medium bowl, toss the meat with ½ tablespoon of the sugar, 1 tablespoon of the oil and 1 teaspoon each of salt and pepper. Let stand at room temperature for 1 hour.

2. In a small bowl, whisk the remaining 3 tablespoons of sugar with the soy sauce, fish sauce, vinegar and rice wine, if using.

3. Heat a large skillet until very hot. Add the remaining ⅓ cup of oil and heat until smoking. Add the meat and cook undisturbed over high heat until browned, 1 minute. Turn the meat and cook for 1 minute longer. Tilt the skillet and spoon off all but 1 tablespoon of the oil. Scatter the scallions, onion and garlic over the meat and cook for 30 seconds. Stir the soy mixture and add it to the skillet, shaking to coat the meat; bring to a boil. Add the butter and shake the skillet until melted.

4. Line a platter with watercress and pour the shaking beef and vegetables on top. Serve with lime wedges.
—*Marcia Kiesel*

EDAMAME FRIED BROWN RICE

Active 20 min; Total 1 hr; Serves 4

1 cup uncooked short-grain brown rice

2 cups water

2 Tbsp. extra-virgin olive oil

½ medium onion, diced

3 garlic cloves, minced

2 cups shelled edamame (8 oz.)

1 medium carrot, grated or diced

1 large egg, beaten

2 Tbsp. Asian fish sauce

Freshly cracked black pepper

1. In a medium saucepan, combine the rice with the 2 cups of water and bring to a simmer. Cover, reduce the heat to low and simmer gently for 30 to 40 minutes, until the water is completely absorbed. Remove from the heat, fluff the rice and let cool (or refrigerate) to room temperature.

2. Heat a large skillet over moderate heat. Add the olive oil, onion and garlic and cook until softened, about 2 minutes. Stir in the rice, breaking up any clumps. Cook, stirring constantly, until heated through, about 3 minutes. Stir in the edamame and carrot and cook until heated through, 2 minutes. Stir in the egg and fish sauce until well mixed. Cook, stirring occasionally, until the egg is set, another 2 minutes. Season with black pepper. Serve warm.
—*Todd Porter and Diane Cu*

Suggested Pairing

Serve the beef with an aromatic, medium-bodied California Cabernet Franc.

GRILLED BOK CHOY
WITH BRAISED MUSHROOMS

Active 1 hr; Total 2 hr plus overnight soaking; Serves 4

2½ oz. dried shiitake mushrooms (about 5 cups)

3 Tbsp. canola oil, plus more for brushing

One 1-inch piece of peeled fresh ginger—½ inch smashed, ½ inch cut into thin matchsticks

½ oz. rock sugar, crushed, or 1 Tbsp. granulated sugar

1 scallion, cut into 3-inch lengths

2 cups plus 2 Tbsp. chicken stock or low-sodium broth

¼ cup plus 1 Tbsp. oyster sauce

Kosher salt

1 tsp. unaged whiskey or other grain alcohol

1 lb. bok choy, quartered lengthwise

1. In a large bowl, cover the shiitake with water and let soak overnight at room temperature. Drain the mushrooms and discard the stems.

2. In a large saucepan, heat 2 tablespoons of the oil until shimmering. Add the smashed ginger, sugar and scallion and cook over moderate heat, stirring, until the sugar dissolves and starts to caramelize, 4 to 5 minutes. Add the mushrooms and 2 cups of the chicken stock and bring to a boil. Cover partially and simmer over low heat, stirring occasionally, until the mushrooms are tender and most of the stock has evaporated, 1 hour and 15 minutes. Stir in 1 tablespoon of the oyster sauce and season with salt.

3. Meanwhile, in a small saucepan, heat the remaining 1 tablespoon of canola oil until shimmering. Add the ginger matchsticks and cook over moderately high heat, stirring, until lightly golden, 1 minute. Add the whiskey and cook for 30 seconds. Add the remaining 2 tablespoons of chicken stock and ¼ cup of oyster sauce and simmer over moderately low heat until thickened, about 5 minutes. Keep the ginger oyster sauce warm.

4. In a large pot of salted boiling water, blanch the bok choy until crisp-tender, 2 minutes. Drain and cool under running water; pat dry.

5. Light a grill or heat a grill pan. Brush the bok choy with oil and grill over high heat, turning, until lightly charred, 5 minutes. Transfer to plates or a platter and top with the mushrooms. Drizzle the ginger oyster sauce over the bok choy and mushrooms and serve. —*Bryant Ng*

How to Peel and Mince Ginger

1. Scrape off the skin with the edge of a tablespoon.

2. Slice peeled ginger into thin coins.

3. Then cut into strips.

4. Dice and mince.

Grilled Lamb
+ Pickled Eggplant Salad
+ Spiced Lentils

Chef Timothy Hollingsworth deftly balances Mediterranean flavors with this enticing combination of grilled lamb chops, tender, tangy eggplant salad and herbed yogurt sauce. The earthy flavors of Jill Donenfeld's spiced lentils, shiitake mushrooms and Swiss chard in the stewy side dish complement the grilled lamb and eggplant. The spiced lentil dish can be refrigerated for up to three days.

GRILLED LAMB WITH PICKLED EGGPLANT SALAD AND HERBED YOGURT

Active 1 hr; Total 1 hr 45 min plus 8 hr marinating; Serves 4

LAMB

½ cup extra-virgin olive oil

¼ cup fresh lemon juice

1 Tbsp. minced garlic

1 Tbsp. minced rosemary

1 Tbsp. minced thyme

12 baby lamb chops (3 lbs.)

Kosher salt and pepper

YOGURT SAUCE

1 cup whole-milk yogurt

1 tsp. finely grated lemon zest, plus 1½ Tbsp. fresh lemon juice

1½ tsp. finely chopped thyme

1½ tsp. finely chopped rosemary

Kosher salt and pepper

SALAD

1 cup Champagne vinegar

⅓ cup sugar

¼ cup fresh orange juice

Two 12-oz. Japanese or Chinese eggplants, cut into ½-inch dice

1 English cucumber, chopped

¾ cup pitted mixed marinated olives

2 cups baby arugula

Kosher salt and pepper

1. Marinate the lamb In a baking dish, whisk the olive oil with the lemon juice, garlic, rosemary and thyme. Add the lamb and turn to coat. Cover and refrigerate for 8 hours or overnight, turning occasionally. Bring the lamb to room temperature before grilling.

2. Make the yogurt sauce In a medium bowl, whisk the yogurt with the lemon zest, lemon juice, thyme and rosemary. Season the sauce with salt and pepper.

3. Make the salad In a saucepan, combine the vinegar with the sugar, orange juice and 1 cup of water; bring to a boil over moderately high heat. Add the eggplant and cook for 2 minutes. Off the heat, let the eggplant cool completely in the liquid, about 45 minutes. Drain well.

4. Light a grill or preheat a grill pan. Remove the lamb from the marinade and season with salt and pepper. Grill over high heat, turning once, until charred outside and medium-rare within, about 6 minutes total. Transfer the chops to plates and let rest for 5 minutes.

5. In a bowl, toss the drained pickled eggplant with the cucumber, olives and arugula. Season the salad with salt and pepper. Serve the lamb with the salad, passing the yogurt sauce at the table. —*Timothy Hollingsworth*

MAKE AHEAD The pickled eggplant can be refrigerated for up to 3 days.

SPICED LENTILS WITH MUSHROOMS AND GREENS

Total 40 min; Serves 4

½ cup brown or green lentils

3 Tbsp. extra-virgin olive oil

½ lb. shiitake mushrooms, stems discarded and caps sliced ¼ inch thick

Salt

1 garlic clove, minced

¼ tsp. ground cumin

¼ tsp. ground coriander

¼ tsp. freshly ground black pepper

⅛ tsp. ground turmeric

½ lb. Swiss chard or other tender greens, large stems discarded and leaves coarsely chopped

1 Tbsp. chopped parsley

1. In a small saucepan, cover the lentils with 2½ cups of water and bring to a boil. Cover and cook over low heat until the lentils are tender, about 30 minutes.

2. In a medium saucepan, heat 2 tablespoons olive oil. Add shiitake and season with salt. Cover and cook over moderate heat, stirring, until mushrooms are tender and starting to brown, about 5 minutes. Add remaining 1 tablespoon of olive oil along with garlic, cumin, coriander, pepper and turmeric and cook, stirring, until fragrant, about 1 minute. Add greens and cook, stirring, until wilted, about 2 minutes.

3. Add the lentils and their cooking liquid to the mushrooms and simmer for 3 minutes. Add up to ¼ cup of water if the lentils are too dry. Season with salt. Ladle the lentils into bowls, garnish with the parsley and serve.
—*Jill Donenfeld*

MAKE AHEAD The lentils can be refrigerated for up to 3 days. Reheat gently.

+BONUS RECIPE: DESSERT

FALLEN OLIVE OIL SOUFFLÉ CAKE

Active 20 min; Total 50 min; Serves 4

9 large egg yolks

2 large eggs

½ cup sugar

3 Tbsp. extra-virgin olive oil, plus more for drizzling

1 Tbsp. all-purpose flour

Flaky sea salt, for garnish

1. Preheat the oven to 350°. Line an 8-inch round cake pan with parchment paper, allowing a 3-inch overhang all around. In a bowl, beat the egg yolks, eggs and sugar at medium-high speed until fluffy and doubled in volume, about 6 minutes. With the mixer at low speed, drizzle in 3 tablespoons olive oil, then beat in flour just until incorporated and scrape into prepared pan. Bake until puffed and set around the edge and golden on top but slightly wobbly in the center, 18 to 20 minutes. Transfer the pan to a rack and let the soufflé cool for 10 minutes.

2. Using the parchment, carefully transfer the soufflé to a platter. Drizzle with olive oil, sprinkle with sea salt and serve hot or at room temperature. —*Nuno Mendes*

MAKE AHEAD The soufflé cake can be baked up to 6 hours ahead.

Suggested Wine Pairing

Serve the lamb with a spicy, lightly smoky, full-bodied Shiraz from Australia.

Spiced Lentils with
Mushrooms and Greens

winter

Roasted Brussels Sprout Quiche
+ Tangy Apple Salad
+ Sweet Potato–Squash Gratin

Among chef Billy Allin's favorite cold-weather recipes is this quiche, packed with earthy Gruyère cheese and roasted Brussels sprouts. You can refrigerate the quiche overnight and bring it to room temperature or reheat just before serving. For Melissa Rubel Jacobson's gratin, use a mandoline to cut the vegetables into thin slices; they will become tender when baked with broth and cream. Add sweetness to the menu with Donald Link's apple salad.

ROASTED BRUSSELS SPROUT AND GRUYÈRE QUICHE

Active 30 min; Total 4 hr 30 min; Serves 6

PASTRY

1 cup all-purpose flour

1 cup cake flour

½ tsp. kosher salt

2 sticks chilled unsalted butter, cut into ½-inch cubes

6 Tbsp. ice water

FILLING

¾ lb. Brussels sprouts, quartered

2 Tbsp. extra-virgin olive oil

1½ cups milk

1½ cups heavy cream

4 large egg yolks

3 large eggs

1 tsp. salt

¾ tsp. freshly ground white pepper

⅛ tsp. freshly grated nutmeg

⅓ cup thinly sliced scallions

4 oz. Gruyère cheese, shredded (1⅓ cups)

1. Make the pastry In a food processor, pulse both flours with the salt. Add the butter and pulse until the mixture resembles coarse meal. Drizzle the ice water on top and pulse until the dough just comes together. Turn the dough out onto a work surface, gather up any crumbs and pat the dough into a disk. Wrap in plastic and refrigerate until well chilled, about 1 hour.

2. On a lightly floured work surface, roll out the dough to a 14-inch round, ¼ inch thick. Ease the dough into a 9-inch round, 2-inch-deep cake pan; do not trim the overhanging dough. Refrigerate until firm, about 30 minutes.

3. Preheat the oven to 350°. Line the pastry with parchment paper and fill with pie weights. Bake for 20 minutes, until barely set. Remove the parchment and pie weights. Bake for 15 to 20 minutes, until lightly browned. Let cool on a rack. Increase the oven temperature to 425°.

4. Make the filling On a rimmed baking sheet, toss the Brussels sprouts with the olive oil. Roast in the oven for about 20 minutes, tossing once, until browned and tender. Let cool, then coarsely chop. Reduce the oven temperature to 325°.

5. In a medium bowl, whisk the milk with the cream, egg yolks, eggs, salt, white pepper and nutmeg. Stir in the Brussels sprouts and scallions. Sprinkle the Gruyère in the crust and pour the filling on top. Set the cake pan on a foil-lined baking sheet and bake the quiche for about 1½ hours, until set. Transfer to a rack and let cool for 30 minutes. Using a paring knife, trim the excess crust and discard. Cut the quiche into wedges and serve. —*Billy Allin*

SWEET POTATO–SQUASH GRATIN

Active 25 min; Total 2 hr 15 min; Serves 6 to 8

2 large sweet potatoes, peeled

1 butternut squash neck (2¼ lbs.) from a large butternut squash, peeled

1 medium rutabaga (2 lbs.), peeled and halved lengthwise

Kosher salt and pepper

½ cup low-sodium chicken broth

¼ cup heavy cream

¾ cup panko (Japanese breadcrumbs)

1½ Tbsp. extra-virgin olive oil

1. Preheat the oven to 375°. Using a mandoline, slice the sweet potatoes and squash lengthwise ⅛ inch thick. Slice the rutabaga crosswise ⅛ inch thick.

2. Spray an 8-by-12-inch cast-iron baking pan with cooking spray. Arrange half of the sweet potatoes in the dish, overlapping them slightly; season with salt and pepper. Top with half of the rutabaga and squash, seasoning each layer. Repeat the layering. Pour the broth over and around the vegetables.

3. Cover tightly with foil and bake for 1 hour, until the vegetables are almost tender when pierced. Remove the foil and pour the cream over the gratin. Bake for about 30 minutes longer, until the liquid has thickened.

4. Preheat the broiler. In a small bowl, mix the panko with the oil and season with salt and pepper; sprinkle over the gratin. Broil 3 inches from the heat for 2 minutes, until golden, rotating for even browning. Let the gratin stand for 10 minutes, then serve. —*Melissa Rubel Jacobson*

TANGY APPLE SALAD

Total 15 min; Serves 6

2 tsp. cider vinegar

Pinch of sugar

¼ cup buttermilk

¼ cup vegetable oil

Kosher salt and freshly ground black pepper

2 large Granny Smith apples, peeled and cut into thin matchsticks

Two 6-oz. bunches of watercress, thick stems discarded

In a large bowl, whisk the cider vinegar with the sugar and buttermilk. Gradually whisk in the vegetable oil and season the cider dressing with salt and pepper. Add the apple matchsticks and watercress and toss to coat. Serve the apple salad right away. —*Donald Link*

MAKE AHEAD The dressing can be refrigerated overnight.

Suggested Pairing

Serve the quiche with a vibrant, full-bodied white such as a Pouilly-Fuisse from France.

Gruyère Cheese Soufflé
+ Sautéed Carrots
+ Endive Salad

To get the most crust with the cheesiest flavor, master chef Jacques Pépin uses a wide, shallow gratin dish, then creates a lattice on top with thin slices of American cheese. A soufflé ramekin would work just as well. Simple side dishes for the cheese soufflé include sautéed carrots flavored with fresh marjoram and lemon juice plus chef Daniel Holzman's fresh endive salad with crisp pears and crunchy pumpkin seeds.

GRUYÈRE CHEESE SOUFFLÉ
Active 25 min; Total 1 hr; Serves 4

3 Tbsp. unsalted butter, plus more for greasing

2 Tbsp. freshly grated Parmigiano-Reggiano cheese

3½ Tbsp. all-purpose flour

1 cup cold whole milk

5 large eggs, separated

½ tsp. kosher salt

½ tsp. freshly ground pepper

3 oz. Gruyère cheese, shredded (1 cup)

2 Tbsp. chopped chives

2 slices of yellow American cheese, each cut into 6 strips

1. Preheat the oven to 400°. Grease a 1-quart gratin dish with butter and dust with the Parmigiano; refrigerate. In a saucepan, melt the 3 tablespoons of butter over moderate heat. Whisk in the flour and cook, whisking, for 1 minute. Whisk in the milk, bring to a boil and cook, whisking, until thickened, 1 minute. Remove the béchamel from the heat, then whisk in 4 egg yolks along with the salt and pepper; reserve the remaining yolk for another use.

2. In a clean bowl, beat the whites until firm peaks form. Whisk one-third of the whites into the béchamel, then fold in the remaining beaten whites. Fold in the Gruyère and chives; scrape into the prepared dish. Arrange the American cheese strips on top in a crisscross pattern. Bake for 25 minutes, until puffed and golden. Serve.

—Jacques Pépin

Jacques Pépin's Tips for a No-Fail Soufflé

A puffy soufflé can seem like a small miracle. For the basics of making one, legendary French chef Jacques Pépin provides these insights.

BEAT IN A COPPER BOWL According to Pépin, the metal interacts with the egg whites to make them more stable as they take on air.

BEAT AT THE RIGHT SPEED "Start beating the egg whites fast to make them more liquid," Pépin says. "Then slow down—lifting them with the whisk, and not touching the bowl too much."

BE PREPARED FOR OVERFLOW Egg whites can yield different volumes when beaten. "Sometimes there's extra that won't fit in the dish—that's OK," says Pépin.

BAKE THE SOUFFLÉ IMMEDIATELY For Pépin, the most important thing when working with beaten egg whites is the timing: Use them right away, he warns, or they'll deflate.

SAUTÉED CARROTS WITH LEMON AND MARJORAM

Total 30 min; Serves 4

3 Tbsp. extra-virgin olive oil

1 large garlic clove, minced

2 lbs. carrots (about 16), cut diagonally into ½-inch slices

1 tsp. sugar

½ tsp. salt

¼ tsp. freshly ground black pepper

1 Tbsp. chopped fresh marjoram

4 tsp. fresh lemon juice

1. In a large nonstick skillet, heat 1½ tablespoons of oil over moderately low heat. Add garlic, carrots, sugar, ¼ teaspoon salt, pepper and marjoram. Cover and cook 5 minutes.

2. Remove cover from the skillet, increase heat to moderate and cook, stirring frequently, until carrots are tender and beginning to brown, about 8 minutes. Remove from heat; stir in lemon juice, remaiing 1½ tablespoons oil and ¼ teaspoon salt.

ENDIVE SALAD WITH PEARS AND PUMPKIN SEEDS

Total 30 min; Serves 4 to 6

VINAIGRETTE

3 Tbsp. red wine vinegar

1 Tbsp. fresh lemon juice

2 tsp. Dijon mustard

2 tsp. honey

½ cup extra-virgin olive oil

Kosher salt

SALAD

1 Tbsp. extra-virgin olive oil

½ cup pumpkin seeds

Kosher salt

3 Belgian endives (1 lb.), cored and sliced 1 inch thick

1 head of frisée (8 oz.), core and dark green leaves discarded, white and light green leaves chopped into 2-inch pieces (8 cups)

1 large red d'Anjou pear—cored, quartered and thinly sliced

3 scallions, thinly sliced on the diagonal

1. Make the vinaigrette In a medium bowl, combine the vinegar, lemon juice, mustard and honey. While whisking constantly, slowly drizzle in the oil until well emulsified. Season with salt.

2. Make the salad In a small skillet, heat the olive oil. Toast the pumpkin seeds over moderate heat, stirring, until golden, 2 to 3 minutes. Transfer to a paper towel–lined plate to drain; season with salt.

3. In a large bowl, toss the endives, frisée, pear and scallions with half of the vinaigrette and season with salt. Transfer the salad to plates and top with the pumpkin seeds. Serve the remaining vinaigrette on the side.
—*Daniel Holzman*

Suggested Pairing

A full-bodied Champagne is a lovely match for the soufflé.

Cumin Chili

+ Jicama Salad
+ Scallion Corn Bread

Cumin-scented beef and bean chili will kick winter's chill. For a hotter chili, add as much cayenne as you like. Serve with Paula Disbrowe's homemade corn bread and a crisp jicama salad from chef Tom Colicchio. To keep the jicama crisp, start with a very firm root and cut the julienne a bit thicker than you usually would.

CUMIN CHILI

Active 10 min; Total 45 min; Serves 4

1½ Tbsp. vegetable oil

1 onion, chopped

1 green bell pepper, chopped

3 garlic cloves, minced

1½ lbs. ground beef

One 28-oz. can whole tomatoes,
crushed by hand and juices reserved

2 Tbsp. tomato paste

1 Tbsp. ground cumin

1 tsp. dried oregano

1 tsp. salt

¼ tsp. freshly ground black pepper

One 15-oz. can pinto or kidney beans,
drained and rinsed

1. In a large saucepan, heat the oil over moderately low heat. Add the onion, bell pepper and garlic and cook, stirring, until the vegetables start to soften, about 10 minutes. Increase the heat to moderate. Add the ground beef and cook, stirring, until the meat is no longer pink, about 5 minutes.

2. Stir in the tomatoes with their juices, the tomato paste, cumin, oregano, salt and pepper and bring to a simmer. Reduce the heat and simmer, partially covered, for 10 minutes. Add the beans and simmer, partially covered, until the vegetables are tender and the chili is thickened, about 5 minutes longer.

VARIATION Add one 10-oz. package of thawed frozen corn to the chili along with the beans.

Guide to Chiles

POBLANO These chiles can grow up to 6 inches long. Young ones are mild and dark green; mature ones turn red and hotter. Poblanos can be fried or stuffed, and are used for chiles en nogada.
Heat: Mild

JALAPEÑO Jalapeños are most often sold green, but red ones, which are slightly hotter and sweeter, are also available. They're great roasted, pickled or raw in salsas, salads and as a garnish.
Heat: Mild to moderate

THAI Thin-skinned and small, Thai chiles can be red or green. They're a spicy and colorful garnish for soups and stews.
Heat: Very hot

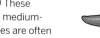

FRESNO These small to medium-size chiles are often mistaken for jalapeños. Younger Fresnos are green and mild; mature peppers are orange and red, with more heat. Raw or roasted Fresnos are terrific in salsas.
Heat: Mild to moderate

SERRANO These fleshy chiles can be red, orange, yellow, green or brown. They're excellent in pico de gallo and other salsas.
Heat: Moderate to hot

HABANERO These small, squat chiles are generally orange or red. They're fantastic in salsas and hot sauces.
Heat: Very hot

JICAMA SALAD

Total 30 min; Serves 4 to 6

One 1½-lb. jicama, peeled and julienned

2 celery ribs, thinly sliced

1 Fresno chile, thinly sliced

⅓ cup fresh lime juice

¼ cup extra-virgin olive oil

½ cup torn basil leaves

Kosher salt

Combine all of the ingredients in a large bowl and let the jicama salad stand for 15 minutes. Serve. —*Tom Colicchio*

CORN BREAD WITH SCALLIONS

Active 10 min; Total 40 min; Serves 4 to 6

1⅓ cups all-purpose flour

1 cup coarse, stone-ground yellow cornmeal

2 tsp. baking powder

1 tsp. salt

Pinch of freshly ground pepper

1¼ cups low-fat milk

2 Tbsp. honey

2 large eggs, beaten

⅓ cup plus 1 Tbsp. corn oil

8 scallions, white and tender green parts only, thinly sliced

1. Preheat the oven to 400°. Place a 10-inch cast-iron skillet in the oven to heat. In a medium bowl, whisk the flour, cornmeal, baking powder, salt and pepper. In a small bowl, whisk the milk, honey, eggs and ⅓ cup of the oil. Add the wet ingredients to the cornmeal mixture and whisk just until combined. Stir in the scallions.

2. Add the remaining 1 tablespoon of oil to the hot skillet and swirl to coat. Pour the batter into the skillet and bake for about 30 minutes, until the top is golden and a toothpick inserted in the center comes out clean. Let cool slightly, then turn the corn bread out onto a plate. Invert it onto a rack to cool. Alternatively, serve the corn bread hot from the skillet. —*Paula Disbrowe*

+BONUS RECIPE: DESSERT

DOUBLE-CHOCOLATE COOKIE CRUMBLE

Active 20 min; Total 50 min; Makes 9 cups

½ lb. dark chocolate (72 percent), coarsely chopped

1¾ cups all-purpose flour

⅓ cup oat flour

¼ cup plus 2 Tbsp. unsweetened cocoa powder

2 tsp. baking soda

1¼ tsp. kosher salt

2 sticks unsalted butter, at room temperature

1 cup turbinado sugar

⅓ cup plus 1 Tbsp. granulated sugar

Vanilla ice cream, for serving

1. In a food processor, pulse the chocolate until it is the size of peas. Transfer to a plate and freeze for 30 minutes.

2. Preheat the oven to 325°. Line 2 rimmed baking sheets with parchment paper. Sift both flours with the cocoa powder, baking soda and salt. In a large bowl, using an electric mixer, beat the butter with both sugars at medium speed until very light and fluffy, 5 minutes. Beat in the flour mixture just until incorporated, then stir in the frozen chocolate.

3. Drop almond-sized clumps of the dough in a single layer onto the prepared baking sheets; the dough will look crumbly and uneven. Bake for 8 to 10 minutes, until the top is dry but the crumble is still soft. Let cool completely. Serve over ice cream. —*Nicole Krasinski*

Suggested Pairing

Serve a jammy California Red Zinfandel with the chili.

Suggested Pairing

Pair this creamy stew with a lime-scented dry Riesling from Australia.

Chickpea Vegetable Stew
+ Warm Lentil Salad
+ Feta-and-Radish Toasts

Chef Cathal Armstrong gives this meatless vegetable stew heft with fingerling potatoes and chickpeas, creaminess with coconut milk and subtle heat with harissa. A warm salad featuring multicolored carrots, sliced parsnips and lentils from Whitney Tingle and Danielle DuBoise is a hearty accompaniment with the vegetable stew. Serve with savory feta-radish toasts created by Steven Satterfield.

CHICKPEA VEGETABLE STEW
Total 35 min; Serves 4

2 Tbsp. extra-virgin olive oil

1 cup frozen pearl onions, thawed and halved

1 red bell pepper, diced

½ lb. fingerling potatoes, halved lengthwise

2 garlic cloves, minced

1 Tbsp. finely chopped peeled fresh ginger

1 Tbsp. harissa

3 cups chicken stock or low-sodium broth

One 15-oz. can chickpeas, drained and rinsed

¾ cup unsweetened coconut milk

2 Tbsp. fresh lemon juice

Kosher salt and pepper

1 Tbsp. minced cilantro

Toasted bread, for serving

1. In a large saucepan, heat the olive oil. Add the onions and bell pepper and cook over moderately high heat, stirring, until browned, about 5 minutes. Add the potatoes, garlic, ginger and harissa and cook, stirring, until the harissa darkens, about 2 minutes. Add the stock and chickpeas and bring to a boil. Cover and simmer over moderately low heat until the potatoes are tender, 12 to 14 minutes.

2. Add the coconut milk and bring to a simmer. Stir in the lemon juice and season with salt and pepper. Sprinkle the stew with the cilantro and serve with toasted bread.

—Cathal Armstrong

3 Ways to Use Chickpeas

HUMMUS In a food processor, combine one 15-ounce can of drained chickpeas with 1 tablespoon of the liquid, 1 garlic clove, 1 tablespoon of lemon juice and ¼ cup of tahini; puree to a chunky paste. Add 2 tablespoons of olive oil and a pinch of paprika and puree until smooth. Season the hummus with salt, drizzle with olive oil and serve with pita chips or crudités.

SALAD Combine one 15-ounce can of rinsed chickpeas with 3 cups of cooked and cooled quinoa, 4 ounces of baby spinach, 2 chopped tomatoes and 3 chopped scallions. Add 2 ounces of crumbled feta and 3 tablespoons each of fresh lemon juice and olive oil; toss gently but thoroughly to combine. Season to taste with salt and pepper and serve.

SANDWICHES Gently mash one 15-ounce can of rinsed chickpeas with a fork. Stir in 2 tablespoons each of mayonnaise and minced red onion and 1 tablespoon each of fresh lemon juice and chopped dill; season with salt and pepper. Spoon the salad onto 4 slices of multigrain toast and top with sliced avocado and radish or alfalfa sprouts. Close the sandwiches with 4 more slices of toast and serve.

WARM LENTIL AND ROOT VEGETABLE SALAD WITH COCONUT TZATZIKI

Active 30 min; Total 1 hr 15 min; Serves 4 to 6

LENTILS

1 cup French green lentils, picked over

Fine Himalayan pink salt and pepper

1½ lbs. medium multicolored carrots, cut on a bias into 2-inch pieces

1½ lbs. medium parsnips, halved lengthwise and cut into 2-inch pieces

2¼ tsp. ground cumin

2¼ tsp. ground coriander

½ tsp. ancho chile powder

½ cup plus 2 Tbsp. extra-virgin olive oil

⅓ cup fresh lemon juice

¾ cup chopped mint, plus torn leaves for garnish

¾ cup chopped cilantro, plus leaves for garnish

TZATZIKI

1 cup coconut milk yogurt

¼ cup finely diced seeded cucumber

1 Tbsp. extra-virgin olive oil

1 Tbsp. fresh lemon juice

1 tsp. finely chopped dill

1 tsp. finely chopped chives

1 garlic clove, minced

Fine Himalayan pink salt and pepper

1. Make the lentils In a large saucepan, cover the lentils with 2 inches of water and bring to a boil. Simmer over moderate heat until just tender, 20 minutes. Remove from the heat, add a generous pinch of salt and let stand for 5 minutes; drain. Spread the lentils on a rimmed baking sheet and let cool slightly.

2. Meanwhile, preheat the oven to 400°. On a large rimmed baking sheet, toss the carrots and parsnips with the cumin, coriander, chile powder and ¼ cup of the olive oil. Season generously with salt and pepper. Roast the vegetables until tender and browned in spots, 20 to 25 minutes.

3. In a large bowl, toss the lentils with the warm roasted vegetables, the lemon juice and the remaining ¼ cup plus 2 tablespoons of olive oil. Fold in the chopped mint and cilantro and season the salad with salt and pepper. Transfer to a platter and garnish with mint and cilantro leaves.

4. Make the tzatziki In a small bowl, whisk all of the ingredients together and season with salt and pepper. Serve alongside the warm lentil salad.
—*Whitney Tingle and Danielle DuBoise*

FETA-AND-RADISH TOASTS

Total 20 min; Serves 4

4½-inch-thick slices of peasant bread

2 Tbsp. extra-virgin olive oil, plus more for drizzling

3 oz. feta cheese (preferably goat), crumbled

4 to 5 radishes, thinly sliced

½ bunch watercress, thick stems discarded

Salt and freshly ground pepper

Heat a cast-iron grill pan. Brush the bread with 2 tablespoons of the olive oil and grill over high heat, turning once, until toasted. Top the toasts with the feta, radishes and watercress. Drizzle with olive oil, sprinkle with salt and pepper and serve. —*Steven Satterfield*

Warm Lentil and Root Vegetable Salad with Coconut Tzatziki

Italian Seafood Stew

+ Rosemary-Roasted Potatoes
+ Celery, Fennel and Apple Salad

For this luscious tomato-rich stew, chef Marco Canora cooks squid slowly until it becomes tender. He says that squid is essential to the success of the dish because it releases its liquid as it simmers and adds a delicate sweetness to the sauce. Serve the hearty stew with Eugenia Bone's roasted potatoes and a sweet-tart apple salad from Athena Calderone.

ITALIAN SEAFOOD STEW

Active 1 hr; Total 2 hr; Serves 6

½ cup extra-virgin olive oil, plus more for drizzling

1 fennel bulb, cored and finely chopped

2 celery ribs, finely chopped

1 white onion, finely chopped

1 Tbsp. dried oregano (preferably Sicilian)

Pinch of crushed red pepper

1½ lbs. cleaned squid, bodies cut into ½-inch rings, tentacles halved

2 cups dry white wine

One 28-oz. can tomato puree

2 lemons—zest of one peeled in strips with a vegetable peeler, zest of the other finely grated

Kosher salt and freshly ground black pepper

1 cup bottled clam juice

12 oz. mussels, scrubbed

12 oz. littleneck clams, scrubbed

12 oz. shelled and deveined large shrimp

12 oz. skinless striped bass fillet, cut into 2-by-1-inch pieces

2 Tbsp. finely chopped flat-leaf parsley

1. In a very large, enameled cast-iron casserole or Dutch oven, heat the ½ cup of olive oil. Add the fennel, celery, onion, oregano and crushed red pepper and cook over moderate heat, stirring frequently, until the vegetables are softened, about 15 minutes. Add the squid and cook over moderately low heat for another 15 minutes, stirring occasionally.

2. Stir in the wine and bring to a boil over moderately high heat. Cook until evaporated, about 20 minutes. Stir in the tomato puree and strips of lemon zest. Season with salt and pepper and cook over very low heat, stirring occasionally, until very thick, about 40 minutes.

3. Add the clam juice and 2 cups of water and bring to a boil. Remove and discard the lemon zest. Season the broth with salt and pepper. Add the mussels, clams and shrimp, cover and cook until most of the shells have opened, about 5 minutes. Add the striped bass and cook until opaque, about 2 minutes longer. Discard any unopened mussels and clams.

4. In a small bowl, combine the parsley with the grated lemon zest. Spoon the stew into deep bowls and sprinkle with the gremolata. Drizzle with olive oil and serve.
—*Marco Canora*

MAKE AHEAD The recipe can be prepared through Step 2 and refrigerated overnight. Reheat before proceeding.

Suggested Pairing

Serve the seafood stew with a bright, minerally Italian white from Liguria.

ROSEMARY-ROASTED POTATOES

Active 10 min; Total 1 hr; Serves 6 to 8

2½ lbs. fingerling potatoes, halved lengthwise

3 Tbsp. olive oil

Kosher salt

2 rosemary sprigs

Preheat the oven to 400°. In a roasting pan, toss the potatoes with the olive oil. Season with salt and nestle the rosemary sprigs into the potatoes. Roast for 30 minutes, then flip the potatoes; they should be golden brown. If they stick, don't loosen them. After they cook a few minutes more, you'll be able to flip them over. Roast for another 15 minutes and serve. —*Eugenia Bone*

CELERY, FENNEL AND APPLE SALAD WITH PECORINO AND WALNUTS

Total 30 min; Serves 4 to 6

¾ cup walnuts

3 Tbsp. extra-virgin olive oil, plus more for drizzling

2 Tbsp. fresh lemon juice

Kosher salt and pepper

3 celery ribs, sliced diagonally ¼ inch thick

2 fennel bulbs—trimmed, halved, cored and thinly sliced on a mandoline

2 Honeycrisp apples—halved, cored and sliced

½ cup basil leaves, torn if large

Pecorino cheese shavings, for garnish

1. Preheat the oven to 375°. Spread the walnuts in a pie plate and toast for 7 to 8 minutes, until golden. Coarsely chop the nuts.

2. In a large bowl, whisk the 3 tablespoons of olive oil with the lemon juice and season with salt and pepper. Add the celery, fennel, apples and basil and toss to evenly coat. Transfer the salad to a serving platter. Season with pepper and drizzle with olive oil, then top with the walnuts and garnish with cheese shavings. —*Athena Calderone*

+BONUS RECIPE: COCKTAIL
CAMPARI-FENNEL APERITIF

Total 15 min; Makes 1 drink

Handful of fennel fronds, plus 1 small sprig for garnish

3 lemon wheels

2 oz. dry sparkling wine

¾ oz. Campari

½ oz. simple syrup (see Note)

Ice

One 2-inch-long strip of lemon peel

In a cocktail shaker, combine the fennel fronds, lemon wheels, sparkling wine, Campari and simple syrup. Muddle 20 times. Add ice and shake well. Strain into an ice-filled rocks glass. Squeeze the lemon peel over the drink and add it to the glass. Garnish with the fennel sprig and serve. —*Neal Bodenheimer*

NOTE To make simple syrup, simmer ½ cup water with ½ cup sugar in a small saucepan over moderate heat, stirring until the sugar has dissolved. Let the syrup cool.

Spicy Green Posole
+ Jicama and Citrus Salad
+ Spicy Guacamole

This posole from chef Richard Blais gets its smoky sizzle from tomatillos, poblanos and jalapeños. Be sure to serve the fragrant chicken stew with all of the delicious garnishes suggested. You can pick up fixings for the crunchy citrus salad at the market and make the simplest of all dressings with just citrus juices, salt and pepper. While the posole simmers, dip some chips into a bowl of spicy guacamole from Todd Porter and Diane Cu.

SPICY GREEN POSOLE
Active 45 min; Total 1 hr 20 min ; Serves 4 to 6

1 lb. tomatillos, husked

2 medium poblano chiles

2 jalapeños

2 Tbsp. extra-virgin olive oil

4 chicken thighs (1 lb.)

1 small onion, diced

4 garlic cloves, minced

Two 15-oz. cans hominy, drained and rinsed

5 cups chicken stock

Kosher salt and pepper

Sliced cabbage, radishes and scallions, cilantro, watercress or purslane, Mexican crema and lime wedges, for serving

1. Preheat the broiler and position a rack 4 to 6 inches from the heat. Spread the tomatillos, poblanos and jalapeños on a rimmed baking sheet. Broil for about 10 minutes, turning occasionally, until charred. Transfer to a work surface, then peel and seed the chiles. Finely chop the chiles and tomatillos.

2. Meanwhile, in a large saucepan, heat the oil over moderately high heat. Add the chicken and cook, turning once, until browned, about 10 minutes. Add the onion and garlic and cook, stirring, until translucent, about 3 minutes. Add the tomatillos, chiles, hominy and stock. Bring to a boil, then reduce the heat and simmer for 45 minutes, until the chicken is tender. Season the chicken mixture with salt and pepper.

3. Transfer the chicken to a work surface and shred the meat with a fork; discard the skin and bones. Return the chicken to the soup and simmer until heated through. Serve the posole with cabbage, radishes, scallions, cilantro, watercress, crema and lime wedges. —*Richard Blais*

What to Do with Hominy

Inside a can of hominy you'll find plump, puffy kernels with a wonderfully chewy texture. Start with rinsed and drained hominy for the recipe ideas here.

SALAD Combine hominy with cooked shrimp, halved cherry tomatoes, cilantro, avocado and baby arugula. Toss with a cumin-lime vinaigrette and top with Cotija cheese.

SOUP Swap in hominy for pasta in minestrone. Or add it to Latin soups like Mexican tortilla or black bean soup.

CHILI Replace some (or all!) of the canned beans in your favorite chili with hominy.

JICAMA AND CITRUS SALAD

Total 25 min; Serves 4 to 6

2 Ruby Red grapefruits

2 navel oranges

One 1-lb. jicama, peeled and cut into ½-inch dice

4 radishes, thinly sliced

2 Tbsp. fresh lime juice

¾ cup lightly packed cilantro, chopped

Salt and pepper

Using a very sharp knife, peel the grapefruits and oranges, being sure to remove any bitter white pith. Working over a large bowl to catch the juices, cut in between the membranes to release the sections into the bowl. Cut the citrus into pieces. Add all of the remaining ingredients to the bowl and toss well. Serve the salad right away.

SPICY GUACAMOLE

Total 15 min; Serves 4 to 6

3 large ripe Hass avocados, halved, pitted, and scooped out

1 tsp. fresh lime juice

2 Tbsp. minced cilantro

1 medium jalapeño, seeded and minced

½ tsp. crushed red chili flakes

¼ tsp. Kosher or sea salt

Fresh cracked black pepper

1 medium tomato, seeded and diced

1. In a bowl, mash the avocado with a fork until it is nearly at your desired consistency. Stir in the lime juice, cilantro, jalapeño, chili flakes, salt and pepper.

2. Gently fold in the tomato. Serve immediately or press a piece of plastic wrap flush into the top of the guacamole, refrigerate, and serve preferably within 24 hours.
—*Todd Porter and Diane Cu*

+BONUS RECIPE: COCKTAIL
BREWSKY SANGRIA

Total 10 min; Makes 8 drinks

2 Bartlett pears, peeled and chopped

1 cup plus 2 Tbsp. fresh lemon juice

Four 12-oz. bottles lager, chilled

1 cup triple sec

Ice

2 Bosc pears, sliced, for garnish

1. In a food processor, combine the Bartlett pears with 2 tablespoons of the lemon juice and process to a puree.

2. Slowly pour the beer into a pitcher. Stir in the remaining 1 cup of lemon juice, the triple sec and the pear puree. Fill pint glasses halfway with ice. Add the sangria and garnish with the Bosc pear slices. —*Roger Kugler*

Chicken Roasted on Bread
+ Roasted Carrots
+ Baked Onions

In this simple dish from F&W's Justin Chapple, chicken legs roast atop torn pieces of bread that absorb the rich and tangy juices, becoming deliciously crisp and chewy. In Kay Chun's roasted carrots, chopped carrot greens turn into a tasty topping for sweet carrots and shallots. And the simple, stuffed onions from Nancy Silverton are baked in the oven until they're sweet and tender, then topped with fennel breadcrumbs.

CHICKEN ROASTED ON BREAD WITH CAPERBERRIES AND CHARRED LEMONS

Active 20 min; Total 1 hr 10 min; Serves 4

½ lb. sourdough bread, torn into bite-size pieces

4 large shallots, quartered lengthwise

¾ cup drained caperberries

2 lemons, scrubbed and quartered lengthwise

¼ cup extra-virgin olive oil, plus more for brushing

Kosher salt and pepper

Four 12-oz. whole chicken legs

Preheat the oven to 400°. On a large rimmed baking sheet, toss bread with shallots, caperberries, lemons and ¼ cup olive oil; season with salt and pepper. Brush chicken legs with oil and season with salt and pepper. Arrange the chicken on the bread and roast for about 50 minutes, until the bread is crisp and an instant-read thermometer inserted in the thighs registers 160°. Transfer the chicken, bread and vegetables to plates and serve.

—Justin Chapple

Know Your Capers

Capers are a great way to add deliciously briny flavor to a range of dishes. Here's a guide to the different types.

NONPAREIL CAPERS in brine The smallest of the capers, nonpareils ("having no equal") are the mildest in flavor and can be found jarred in a vinegar brine. They are a key ingredient in veal or chicken piccata as well as pasta puttanesca.

SALT-PACKED CAPERS Prized by aficionados, salt-packed capers are bigger than nonpareils and have a more intense, floral flavor than vinegar-brined varieties. The ones from Pantelleria in Sicily's Lipari Islands are considered the best. Salt-packed capers should be rinsed and soaked in water a few times before being added to dishes. They're fabulous fried until crisp to garnish fish recipes or to simply snack on. Look for them at specialty markets.

CAPERBERRIES When caper buds aren't picked from the plant, they blossom into seed-filled caperberries. They're often found with their stems attached, swimming in brine in the antipasto bar or packed in jars at markets. These bigger, grape-sized berries taste milder than caper buds. They're excellent in place of olives in salads, as a garnish for martinis and Bloody Marys or on a relish plate.

CURRY-ROASTED CARROTS WITH CARROT TOP GREMOLATA

Total 40 min; Serves 4

3 bunches small carrots with tops (2 lbs.), scrubbed and tops reserved

2 large shallots, thinly sliced

3 Tbsp. extra-virgin olive oil

2 tsp. curry powder

Kosher salt and freshly ground pepper

2 Tbsp. fresh lemon juice

¼ cup chopped cilantro

1 tsp. finely grated lemon zest

½ jalapeño, minced

1. Preheat the oven to 425°. On a baking sheet, toss the carrots and shallots with the olive oil and curry powder and season with salt and pepper. Roast for 20 to 25 minutes, stirring occasionally, until the carrots are tender and golden. Drizzle with the lemon juice and toss to coat. Transfer the carrots and shallots to a platter.

2. Meanwhile, in a small bowl, combine the cilantro, lemon zest and jalapeño. Finely chop the carrot tops until you have ½ cup and add to the bowl.

3. Sprinkle the gremolata over the carrots and shallots and serve warm. —Kay Chun

BAKED ONIONS WITH FENNEL BREADCRUMBS

Active 30 min; Total 2 hr 15 min; Serves 4 to 6

3 medium onions, peeled and halved lengthwise, root ends left intact

2 Tbsp. extra-virgin olive oil, plus more for brushing

Kosher salt

½ cup chicken stock

6 bay leaves, preferably fresh

1 tsp. fennel seeds

¼ cup panko (Japanese breadcrumbs)

1½ tsp. minced sage

1. Preheat the oven to 425°. Brush the onion halves with olive oil, season with salt and arrange cut side down in a medium ovenproof skillet. Add the chicken stock and scatter the bay leaves around the onions. Cover tightly with foil and bake for about 1½ hours, until the onions are very tender.

2. Meanwhile, in a small skillet, toast the fennel seeds over moderate heat until fragrant, about 3 minutes. Transfer to a work surface and let cool, then coarsely crush the seeds. Transfer to a small bowl, add the panko, sage and 2 tablespoons of olive oil and toss. Season the fennel breadcrumbs with salt.

3. Carefully turn the onions cut side up in the skillet. Spoon the fennel breadcrumbs on top and bake for about 15 minutes longer, until the crumbs are lightly browned and crisp. Discard the bay leaves and serve the onions hot or warm. —Nancy Silverton

Suggested Pairing

Serve the chicken with a fresh Meyer lemon-scented Sicilian white.

Duck Breasts
+ Apple Cider–Braised Cabbage
+ Roasted Beets

People often think duck is intimidating to cook, but these simply-spiced duck breasts from Richard Betts could not be easier. The roasted beet side dish is chef Tyler Brown's riff on the classic pairing of roasted beets and goat cheese and features goat butter instead of goat cheese. The braised cabbage from chef Tom Colicchio uses both apple cider and apple cider vinegar so the cabbage is fruity and tangy and pairs well with the duck.

FOUR-SPICE DUCK BREASTS
Total 1 hr; Serves 8

1 tsp. coriander seeds

1 tsp. ground cinnamon

1 star anise pod

½ tsp. cumin seeds

Four 10-oz. Muscovy duck breast halves, excess fat removed and skin scored

Kosher salt and freshly ground pepper

1. In a skillet, toast the coriander, cinnamon, star anise and cumin over moderate heat, shaking the skillet, until fragrant, 2 minutes. Transfer the spices to a grinder and let cool, then grind to a powder.

2. Preheat the oven to 400°. Season the duck breasts with salt and pepper and rub all over with the spice mix. Heat a large cast-iron skillet. Add the duck skin side down. Cook over moderate heat, spooning off the fat, until golden and just crisp, about 7 minutes. Turn the duck skin side up. Transfer the skillet to the oven and roast the duck for about 7 minutes, until medium-rare within. Transfer the duck breasts to a carving board and let rest for 5 minutes.

MAKE AHEAD Four 10-ounce duck breast halves will generally serve 8 with a serving size of about 5 ounces. If you have leftover cooked duck, you can store it in an airtight container in the refrigerator for 3 to 4 days and enjoy it for another meal later in the week. —*Richard Betts*

Know Your Duck Varieties

PEKIN Also known as Long Island duckling, this breed features mild-flavored meat that's light in color. In the U.S., it's the chefs' bird of choice for Peking duck and duck à l'orange. The breasts are wonderful pan-seared; this bird also takes well to roasting whole.

MUSCOVY Popular in Europe, Muscovy duck boasts a thin skin on tender meat that's gamier than that of the Pekin. Muscovy ducks are often bred for foie gras, which results not only in an enlarged liver, but also a broad, meaty breast. The flavorful legs are excellent for braises.

MOULARD A cross between a Pekin and Muscovy, this larger breed is also favored for foie gras production. The rich meat has a ruby red color that's deep in flavor. The sizable breasts called magret (from maigre, meaning the lean part of the duck) are prized by the French. They're best grilled or pan-seared until medium-rare. The thick layer of fat under the skin is great for rendering to make duck confit or frying potatoes. The meaty legs are great for braises, stews and for making confit.

APPLE CIDER–BRAISED CABBAGE

Total 1 hr; Serves 4 to 6

2 Tbsp. extra-virgin olive oil

One 1½-lb. head of green cabbage, cut through the core into 6 wedges

½ cup chopped bacon (2 oz.)

1 medium onion, halved through the core and thinly sliced lengthwise

Kosher salt

½ cup cider vinegar

2 cups apple cider

1 Tbsp. unsalted butter

Pepper

1. In a large skillet, heat oil until shimmering. Add cabbage cut side down and cook over moderate heat, turning once, until browned, 6 to 8 minutes. Transfer to a plate.

2. Add bacon to skillet and cook over moderate heat, stirring occasionally, until rendered but not crisp, about 5 minutes. Add onion and a pinch of salt and cook, stirring occasionally, until softened and just starting to brown, about 10 minutes. Stir in vinegar and simmer over moderately high heat until reduced by half, about

3 minutes. Add cider and bring to a boil. Nestle cabbage wedges in skillet, cover and braise over low heat, turning once, until tender, about 20 minutes. Using a slotted spoon, transfer cabbage to a platter and tent with foil.

3. Boil sauce over moderately high heat, stirring occasionally, until slightly thickened, about 5 minutes. Remove skillet from heat and swirl in butter. Season with salt and pepper; spoon over the braised cabbage and serve. —*Tom Colicchio*

ROASTED BEETS AND CELERY ROOT WITH GOAT BUTTER

Active 30 min; Total 1 hr 30 min; Serves 4

1¼ lbs. trimmed baby beets, preferably golden, scrubbed

1 Tbsp. extra-virgin olive oil

3 Tbsp. goat butter

1 lb. celery root, peeled and cut into 2-by-½-inch batons

2 thyme sprigs

Salt and freshly ground pepper

1 cup vegetable stock

1. Preheat the oven to 350°. In a baking dish, toss the beets with the oil. Cover with foil and roast for about 1 hour, until the beets are tender when pierced. Let cool slightly, then peel the beets and cut them into small wedges.

2. In a large, deep skillet, heat 2 tablespoons of goat butter. Add celery root and thyme sprigs and season lightly with salt and pepper. Cook over moderate heat, stirring occasionally, until lightly browned in spots, about 5 minutes. Add ¼ cup of stock and simmer over moderate heat until nearly evaporated, about 2 minutes. Add remaining stock, ¼ cup at a time, and cook until celery root is tender, 8 to 10 minutes total. Stir in beets and cook until heated through, about 2 minutes. Discard thyme sprigs. Swirl in remaining 1 tablespoon of goat butter and season with salt and pepper. —*Tyler Brown*

Suggested Pairing

Try the spiced duck with a black currant-inflected red Bordeaux from France.

Andouille Mac & Cheese

+ Broccoli and Red Onion Roast
+ Bibb Lettuce Salad

Chef Paul Nanni grinds and smokes his own andouille sausage for this Cajun-inspired macaroni and cheese, but you can buy andouille sausage from the local butcher and still get a flavor punch in this hearty pasta dish. To balance the richness of the mac and cheese, offer two savory green vegetables—an earthy roasted broccoli with mushrooms from Marcia Kiesel and a crisp green salad with roasted beets from F&W's Justin Chapple.

ANDOUILLE MAC & CHEESE
Active 1 hr; Total 1 hr 30 min; Serves 4

1½ cups whole milk

1½ cups heavy cream

4 Tbsp. unsalted butter

⅓ cup all-purpose flour

1 garlic clove, minced

½ tsp. finely chopped thyme

Pinch of cayenne

Pinch of freshly grated nutmeg

Pinch of white pepper

1½ cups shredded mild white cheddar (6 oz.)

1½ cups shredded sharp cheddar (6 oz.)

Kosher salt and black pepper

3 Tbsp. canola oil

1 cup panko (Japanese breadcrumbs)

6 oz. andouille sausage, diced

¾ cup finely diced red bell pepper

½ cup finely diced onion

¼ cup thinly sliced scallions, plus more for garnish

¼ cup finely chopped cilantro, plus leaves for garnish

¼ cup finely chopped parsley

1 lb. medium pasta shells

Hot sauce

Thinly sliced hot red chiles or jalapeños, for garnish

1. Preheat oven to 450°. In a small saucepan, bring milk and heavy cream to a simmer. Keep warm over very low heat.

2. In a medium saucepan, melt the butter. Whisk in the flour and cook over moderate heat until bubbling, 1 to 2 minutes. Add the garlic, thyme, cayenne, nutmeg and white pepper and whisk until the roux is lightly browned, 3 to 5 minutes. Gradually whisk in the milk and cream until the sauce is smooth and bring to a boil. Simmer over moderate heat, whisking, until no floury taste remains, 5 to 7 minutes. Remove from the heat and whisk in the mild cheddar and ½ cup of the sharp cheddar. Season the cheese sauce with salt and black pepper.

3. In a large skillet, heat 1 tablespoon of the oil. Add the panko and toast over moderately high heat, stirring, until lightly browned, 3 minutes. Transfer to a plate. Wipe out the skillet.

4. Heat the remaining 2 tablespoons of oil in the skillet. Add the andouille, bell pepper and onion and cook over moderate heat until the vegetables are lightly browned, 5 minutes. Stir in the ¼ cup of sliced scallions and the chopped cilantro and parsley.

5. In a large pot of salted boiling water, cook the pasta until al dente. Drain well, then return the pasta to the pot. Stir in the cheese sauce and the andouille mixture. Season with hot sauce and salt and black pepper.

6. Spoon the pasta into four 12-ounce gratin dishes set on a baking sheet. Top with the remaining 1 cup of sharp cheddar and the toasted panko. Bake until piping hot, 15 to 20 minutes. Let stand for 5 minutes. Garnish with scallions, cilantro and red chiles and serve with hot sauce.

—Paul Nanni

BROCCOLI, SHIITAKE AND RED ONION ROAST

Active 25 min; Total 45 min; Serves 4 to 6

One 1¼-lb. head of broccoli

½ lb. large shiitake mushrooms, stems discarded

1 small red onion, sliced crosswise ⅓ inch thick

Extra-virgin olive oil, for brushing

Salt and freshly ground black pepper

2 Tbsp. balsamic vinegar

Preheat the oven to 425°. Trim and peel the broccoli stems. Cut the broccoli lengthwise into long stalks, with 1 or 2 florets each. Cut any remaining florets into 2-inch pieces. Spread the broccoli on a large, rimmed baking sheet. On another large, rimmed baking sheet, put the shiitake on one side and the onion slices on the other. Generously brush all the vegetables with olive oil, season with salt and pepper and roast for about 20 minutes, until just tender and lightly browned. Transfer the broccoli to a platter. Drizzle the balsamic vinegar over the mushrooms and onion rings and stir to coat the vegetables. Top the broccoli with the shiitake and onion and serve. —*Marcia Kiesel*

BIBB LETTUCE SALAD WITH VINEGAR-ROASTED BEETS

Active 30 min; Total 1 hr 15 min; Serves 6 to 8

1¼ cups plus 3 Tbsp. rice wine vinegar

1¼ cups water

1 Tbsp. sugar

Kosher salt

1½ lbs. small beets

2 thyme sprigs

2 garlic cloves, crushed

1 bay leaf

¾ cup plain yogurt

3 Tbsp. minced shallot

Pepper

Two 8-oz. heads of Bibb lettuce, light green leaves only, large leaves torn

Cilantro leaves and small dill sprigs, for garnish

1. Preheat the oven to 425°. In a large, deep ovenproof skillet, whisk 1¼ cups of the vinegar with the water, sugar and 1 tablespoon of salt. Add the beets, thyme, garlic and bay leaf. Cover the skillet and roast the beets for about 45 minutes, until tender, turning them halfway through. Remove the beets from the skillet and let cool completely, then peel and cut into wedges; discard the cooking liquid.

2. In a medium bowl, whisk the yogurt with the shallot and the remaining 3 tablespoons of vinegar. Season the dressing with salt and pepper.

3. Arrange the lettuce on a platter and top with the beets. Drizzle with half of the dressing and garnish with cilantro leaves and dill sprigs. Serve right away, passing the remaining dressing at the table. —*Justin Chapple*

MAKE AHEAD The drained roasted beets can be refrigerated for up to 3 days.

Suggested Pairing

Serve the mac and cheese with a full-bodied, powerful Chardonnay from Napa Valley.

Sausage and Cheese Lasagna
+ Big Italian Salad
+ Garlic Bread

The rusticity of this gooey lasagna is offset by a touch of fresh basil on top. The salad from Grace Parisi is part green salad, part antipasto salad, and combines lettuce, celery, onion, peperoncini, olives and cherry tomatoes. Serve with warm garlic bread from Laurence Jossel.

Suggested Pairing

Serve a rich, peppery Primitivo from Puglia with the lasagna.

RUSTIC SAUSAGE AND THREE-CHEESE LASAGNA

Active 40 min; Total 2 hr; Serves 6

8 oz. lasagna noodles

3 Tbsp. extra-virgin olive oil, plus more for tossing

8 oz. sweet Italian sausage

4 large garlic cloves, thinly sliced

One 28-oz. can whole tomatoes, chopped, juices reserved

Kosher salt and freshly ground pepper

Unsalted butter, softened

Freshly grated Parmigiano-Reggiano cheese

8 ounces fresh mozzarella, thinly sliced

6 ounces Italian Fontina, thinly sliced

¼ cup thinly sliced basil leaves

1. Preheat the oven to 425°. In a large pot of salted boiling water, cook the lasagna noodles until almost tender, about 5 minutes. Drain and transfer the noodles to a bowl of cold water and let stand for 2 minutes, then drain. Pat the noodles dry. Transfer to a bowl and toss with olive oil.

2. In a medium skillet, heat 1 tablespoon of the olive oil. Add the sausage, cover and cook over moderate heat, turning once, until browned all over. Add 1 cup of water, cover and simmer until the sausage is just cooked through, about 4 minutes.

3. In a large skillet, heat the remaining 2 tablespoons of olive oil. Add the garlic and cook over low heat until golden, about 3 minutes. Add tomatoes with their juices and cook over moderate heat for 10 minutes, stirring occasionally. Add sausage and its poaching liquid; simmer for 4 minutes. Transfer the sausage to a plate. Simmer the sauce over moderate heat until thickened, about 12 minutes. Coarsely break up the sausage and season the sauce with salt and pepper.

4. In a well-buttered 9-by-13-inch ceramic baking dish, arrange 3 lasagna noodles. Spoon a scant ¼ cup of tomato sauce over each lasagna noodle and sprinkle with a little Parmigiano-Reggiano cheese. Top noodles with some of the mozzarella and Fontina and a few chunks of sausage. Repeat the layering process, ending with a layer of noodles. Brush the noodles with butter and sprinkle with Parmigiano-Reggiano.

5. Bake the lasagna on the top rack of the oven for 20 minutes, until the sauce starts to bubble. Increase the oven temperature to 450° and bake for about 7 minutes longer, until the top is richly browned. Let the lasagna rest for about 10 minutes, then scatter the sliced basil on top, cut into squares and serve. —*Marcia Kiesel*

MAKE AHEAD The unbaked lasagna can be refrigerated overnight.

BIG ITALIAN SALAD

Total 30 min; Serves 6

1 garlic clove, smashed

Kosher salt

2 Tbsp. mayonnaise

2 Tbsp. red wine vinegar

½ tsp. dried oregano

¼ cup plus 2 Tbsp. extra-virgin olive oil

Freshly ground pepper

1 large romaine heart, chopped

1 small head of radicchio, halved, cored and coarsely chopped

¼ head of iceberg lettuce, coarsely chopped

1 tender celery rib, thinly sliced

½ small red onion, thinly sliced

½ cup cherry tomatoes

¼ cup pitted green olives, preferably Sicilian

8 peperoncini

2 oz. Parmigiano-Reggiano cheese, shaved (1 cup)

In a large bowl, mash the garlic to a paste with a generous pinch of salt. Whisk in the mayonnaise, vinegar and oregano, then whisk in the olive oil. Season with pepper. Add all of the remaining ingredients and toss well. Serve right away. —*Grace Parisi*

GARLIC BREAD

Total 10 min; Serves 6 to 8

Eight ¾-inch slices of ciabatta

4 Tbsp. unsalted butter

2 large garlic cloves, minced

Kosher salt and freshly ground pepper

¼ cup chopped parsley

1. Preheat the oven to 375°. Arrange the bread slices on a large baking sheet and bake for 6 minutes, until toasted.

2. Meanwhile, in a small skillet, melt the butter. Add the garlic and season with salt and pepper. Cook over moderately low heat until the garlic is golden, about 2 minutes. Stir in the parsley. Spoon the garlic butter over the toasts and serve right away. —*Laurence Jossel*

+BONUS RECIPE: COCKTAIL

CHOCOLATE-RASPBERRY TRUFFLETINI

Total 5 min; Makes 1 drink

2 oz. vanilla vodka

1 oz. Irish cream

¾ oz. Chambord

¾ oz. coffee liqueur

Chocolate shavings

2 raspberries

Fill a cocktail shaker with ice. Add all of the remaining ingredients except the chocolate shavings and berries; shake well. Strain into a chilled martini glass. Garnish with the chocolate and berries. —*Marvin Allen*

Steps for Layering Lasagna

1. Arrange the lasagna noodles in a buttered baking dish.

2. Spoon tomato sauce over each noodle and sprinkle with Parmigiano-Reggiano cheese.

3. Top the noodles with slices of mozzarella and Fontina cheese.

4. Scatter crumbled sausage over the cheese.

5. Repeat the layers. Brush the final noodle layer with butter and sprinkle with Parmigiano-Reggiano.

Pulled Pork Sandwiches
+ Crispy Buffalo Potatoes
+ Red-and-Green Coleslaw

Roasted garlic seasons this pork shoulder, which slow-cooks until it's falling-of-the-bone tender. Shred the meat and top it with a spicy barbecue sauce and crunchy coleslaw for a satisfying sandwich. This classic coleslaw dressed with mayo and sour cream is excellent on its own or piled onto the sandwich. Serve the sandwiches with Kay Chun's crispy potato wedges that are a fun take on Buffalo chicken wings.

PULLED PORK SANDWICHES WITH BARBECUE SAUCE

Active 1 hr 15 min; Total 8 hr 20 min; Serves 8

PULLED PORK

2 heads of garlic, halved crosswise

¼ cup extra-virgin olive oil, plus more for drizzling

Kosher salt and pepper

1 Tbsp. minced thyme

2 tsp. dry mustard

2 tsp. sweet paprika

2 tsp. finely grated peeled fresh ginger

1 tsp. finely grated orange zest

One 5-lb. bone-in pork butt (shoulder roast)

¼ cup packed light brown sugar

¼ cup distilled white vinegar

¼ cup cider vinegar

BARBECUE SAUCE

1¼ cups ketchup

1 cup cola

¼ cup cider vinegar

¼ cup cayenne pepper hot sauce, such as Frank's RedHot

2 Tbsp. unsulfured molasses

2 Tbsp. cornstarch

Split potato buns and Red-and-Green Coleslaw (recipe on page 218), for serving

1. Make the pork Preheat the oven to 350°. Set the garlic cut side up on a sheet of foil, drizzle with oil and season with salt and pepper. Wrap the garlic in the foil and roast for about 1 hour, until very soft. Let cool, then squeeze the garlic cloves out of the skins into a medium bowl. Add the thyme, dry mustard, paprika, ginger, orange zest and the ¼ cup of oil and mash into a paste.

2. Reduce the oven temperature to 300°. Set a rack in a flameproof medium roasting pan and put the pork on it. Season the pork with salt and pepper, then rub it all over with the garlic paste. Cover with foil and roast for 6 hours, until an instant-read thermometer inserted in the thickest part of the meat registers 200°; uncover for the last 45 minutes of cooking. Transfer to a work surface and let cool, then shred. Discard the fat and bones.

3. Spoon off all but 2 tablespoons of fat from the roasting pan. Add the sugar, both vinegars and ½ cup of water to the pan and cook over moderately high heat, whisking, until bubbling and the sugar dissolves, 5 minutes. Add the pork and toss to coat. Season the pork generously with salt and pepper and toss again; keep warm.

4. Meanwhile, make the sauce In a medium saucepan, whisk the ketchup, cola, vinegar, hot sauce, molasses and cornstarch and bring to a boil. Simmer over moderate heat, stirring, until glossy and thick, about 8 minutes; keep warm.

5. Pile the pork on the buns and top with the barbecue sauce and coleslaw. Close the sandwiches and serve.

MAKE AHEAD The recipe can be prepared through Step 4 and refrigerated for up to 4 days. Reheat gently before serving.

CRISPY BUFFALO POTATOES

Active 25 min; Total 1 hr; Serves 8

6 baking potatoes, scrubbed and cut into ½-inch wedges

¼ cup extra-virgin olive oil

Kosher salt and pepper

6 Tbsp. unsalted butter, melted

¼ cup hot sauce

Blue cheese dressing, for serving

1. Preheat the oven to 450°. On 2 rimmed baking sheets, toss the potatoes with the olive oil and season with salt and pepper. Roast for 20 minutes. Flip the potatoes and roast for 15 to 20 minutes longer, until golden and crisp.

2. In a large bowl, combine the butter and hot sauce and season with salt and pepper. Add the potatoes and toss to coat. Serve with blue cheese dressing. —*Kay Chun*

RED-AND-GREEN COLESLAW

Active 15 min; Total 45 min; Serves 8

½ cup sour cream

½ cup mayonnaise

¼ cup distilled white vinegar

2 tsp. turbinado sugar

1 tsp. dry mustard

Kosher salt and pepper

1 lb. green cabbage (½ medium head), cored and very thinly sliced

1 lb. red cabbage (½ medium head), cored and very thinly sliced

In a large bowl, whisk the sour cream with the mayonnaise, vinegar, sugar and dry mustard; season with salt and pepper. Add both cabbages and toss. Cover and refrigerate for 30 minutes. Season with salt and pepper and toss once more before serving.

MAKE AHEAD The coleslaw can be refrigerated overnight.

+BONUS RECIPE: DESSERT
HAZELNUT CHOCOLATE BARS

Active 25 min; Total 1 hr 10 min; Serves 12

2 cups peeled toasted hazelnuts

1 cup confectioners' sugar

1 tsp. pure vanilla extract

½ tsp. pure almond extract

¼ tsp. kosher salt

½ cup light corn syrup

8 oz. dark chocolate, finely chopped

Sprinkles, for garnish

1. In a food processor, pulse the hazelnuts just until finely ground. Add the sugar, vanilla extract, almond extract and salt and pulse to combine. With the machine on, drizzle in the corn syrup and blend until the mixture comes together. Turn the mixture out onto a parchment paper–lined baking sheet and form into a 12-by-2-inch bar. Cut the bar crosswise into 12 equal pieces and freeze until firm, at least 15 minutes.

2. In a microwave-safe medium bowl, melt the chocolate in 30-second intervals, stirring, until smooth. Let cool to room temperature.

3. Using a fork, dip the hazelnut candy into the chocolate to evenly coat, letting the excess drip off. Arrange the bars on the baking sheet and top with sprinkles. Refrigerate until firm, at least 30 minutes. Serve cold. —*Molly Yeh*

MAKE AHEAD The bars can be refrigerated for 5 days.

Suggested Pairing

Serve Blue Point Summer Ale or Sierra Nevada Summerfest beer with the pork sandwiches.

Crispy Buffalo
Potatoes

Meatballs in Tomato Sauce
+ Romaine and Tomato Salad
+ Broccoli Rabe with Black Olives

Chef Daniel Holzman simmers meatballs in sauce without searing them first. "Searing creates a lot of flavor, but you lose a certain subtlety," he says. To make Eugenia Bone's broccoli rabe, look for bunches that are heavy with green flowers, as the leaves are more bitter. For Jordan Carroll's salad, toss lettuce with the oregano vinaigrette before adding the tomatoes and onion.

MEATBALLS IN TOMATO SAUCE
Active 1 hr 30 min; Total 2 hr; Serves 4 to 6

TOMATO SAUCE

½ cup extra-virgin olive oil

1 onion, coarsely chopped (1 cup)

2 carrots, sliced ¾ inch thick (¾ cup)

3 large garlic cloves, crushed

2 Tbsp. tomato paste

1 bay leaf

6 oregano sprigs

Two 28-oz. cans whole peeled San Marzano tomatoes with their juices, crushed by hand

Pinch of crushed red pepper

Kosher salt

MEATBALLS

¾ lb. ground chuck

¾ lb. ground veal

¾ lb. ground pork

½ cup Italian-style dry breadcrumbs (2½ oz.)

¼ cup freshly grated Pecorino Romano cheese (1 oz.)

2 tsp. kosher salt

2 large eggs

½ cup minced onion

½ cup chopped parsley

1 Tbsp. chopped oregano

½ tsp. ground fennel

¼ tsp. crushed red pepper

Freshly grated Grana Padano cheese, for serving

1. Make the tomato sauce In a large ovenproof saucepan, heat the olive oil. Add the onion, carrots and garlic and cook over moderate heat, stirring occasionally, until the onion is softened and translucent, about 8 minutes. Stir in the tomato paste and cook until lightly caramelized, about 3 minutes. Add the bay leaf, oregano, tomatoes and crushed red pepper and bring to a simmer. Cook over moderately low heat, stirring occasionally, until slightly thickened, 15 minutes. Season with salt and keep at a bare simmer.

2. Meanwhile, make the meatballs Preheat oven to 400°. In a large bowl, combine all ingredients except the Grana Padano and mix by hand until well incorporated. Using a 1½-ounce ice cream scoop (3 tablespoons), scoop 24 meatballs (1½ inches in diameter) and roll into neat balls.

3. Add the meatballs to the simmering tomato sauce and bring to a boil. Braise in the oven until firm and cooked through, about 30 minutes. Discard the bay leaf and oregano sprigs. Serve the meatballs and sauce with Grana Padano on the side. *—Daniel Holzman*

SERVE WITH Mashed Yukon Gold potatoes or pasta.

BROCCOLI RABE WITH BLACK OLIVES AND LEMON ZEST

Total 30 min; Serves 4

Two 1-lb. bunches of broccoli rabe, thick stems discarded

2 Tbsp. extra-virgin olive oil, plus more for drizzling

6 garlic cloves, minced

½ tsp. crushed red pepper

½ cup pitted oil-cured black olives, chopped

1 tsp. finely grated lemon zest

Kosher salt

2 Tbsp. freshly grated Parmigiano-Reggiano cheese

1. In a large pot of boiling water, cook the broccoli rabe until it is bright green, about 1 minute. Drain the rabe, reserving ½ cup of the cooking water.

2. In a large skillet, heat the 2 tablespoons of oil. Add the garlic and crushed red pepper and cook over moderately low heat until fragrant, about 1 minute. Add the broccoli rabe and the reserved cooking water, cover and simmer over moderately low heat until tender, about 10 minutes. Stir in the olives and lemon zest and season with salt. Transfer to a serving dish and drizzle with oil. Sprinkle with the cheese and serve. —*Eugenia Bone*

ROMAINE AND TOMATO SALAD

Total 20 min; Serves 4

2 Tbsp. vegetable oil

1 Tbsp. red wine vinegar

¼ tsp. dried oregano, crumbled

Kosher salt and freshly ground pepper

1 large heart of romaine, chopped

¼ cup slivered red onion

4 plum tomatoes (¾ lb.), cut into ½-inch pieces

In a large bowl, whisk the oil with the vinegar and oregano and season with salt and pepper. Add the romaine and toss well. Add the onion and tomatoes and serve right away. —*Jordan Carroll*

Suggested Wine Pairing

Serve meatballs with a concentrated, medium-bodied Italian red such as a Lagrein from Alto Adige.

Pepper-Crusted Prime Rib
+ Accordion Potatoes
+ Creamed Kale

If you're planning to host friends or family for a dinner party, you can't go wrong with prime rib. A mix of soy sauce, ground chile, garlic and peppercorns coats this gorgeous entrée from chef Marcela Valladolid. The rub forms a peppery crust around the juicy meat as it roasts. Kay Chun's crisp, smoky potatoes are a showstopper, but are actually very easy to make, and the creamed kale from chef Tyler Florence is an excellent swap for more traditional creamed spinach. It's served with crispy kale leaves for an impressive presentation.

PEPPER-CRUSTED PRIME RIB ROAST
Active 15 min; Total 4 hr 30 min; Serves 10 to 12

One 9- to 10-lb. prime rib roast

2 Tbsp. kosher salt

¼ cup multicolor whole peppercorns

1 guajillo chile, stemmed and chopped

2 Tbsp. rosemary leaves

¼ cup Dijon mustard

2 Tbsp. all-purpose flour

2 Tbsp. soy sauce

2 Tbsp. Worcestershire sauce

4 garlic cloves, minced

6 cups low-sodium beef broth

1. Season the roast with the salt and let stand at room temperature for 1 hour.

2. In a spice grinder, grind the peppercorns, guajillo chile and rosemary until coarse. Transfer to a medium bowl. Add all of the remaining ingredients except the broth and mix well.

3. Preheat the oven to 400°. Rub the pepper mix all over the roast. Place the roast on a rack set in a roasting pan. Add 2 cups of the broth to the pan and roast for 30 minutes, until the meat is well browned. Add 2 more cups of the broth and loosely tent the roast with foil. Reduce the oven temperature to 350°. Roast for about 2½ hours, until an instant-read thermometer registers 115°; add the remaining 2 cups of broth halfway through. Set the roast on a cutting board to rest for about 30 minutes (the center of the roast will register at 125° for medium-rare).

4. Strain the pan juices into a small saucepan. Skim off as much fat as possible and bring to a simmer. Carve the roast and serve with the pan jus. —*Marcela Valladolid*

Prime Rib Primer

PRIME RIB Prime rib, also known as a standing rib roast, is a perfect cut for a large dinner party. It is cut from the primal rib section of the animal. A whole prime rib is composed of 6 ribs (ribs 6 to 12), which can weigh from 12 to 16 pounds.

BUYING PRIME RIB If such a large roast is too much, ask the butcher for a certain number of ribs instead of a whole roast. Ribs 6 to 9 (also known as the chuck end, second cut, or blade end) are closer to the shoulder and contain more big chunks of fat, whereas ribs 10 to 12 (also known as the loin end, small end, or first cut) are leaner but more more tender. Prime rib can be sold bone-in or boneless, and you can ask the butcher to cut the meat off the bones and tie it back on, which helps in the carving process once the roast is cooked. Plan on approximately one pound of bone-in prime rib per person, or one rib for every two diners.

ACCORDION POTATOES

Active 30 min; Total 1 hr 10 min; Serves 8 to 12

¾ cup extra-virgin olive oil

2 Tbsp. pimentón de la Vera or other sweet paprika

2 lbs. new fingerling potatoes

Kosher salt and freshly ground black pepper

2 bunches small fresh or dried bay leaves

1. Preheat the oven to 375°. In a small bowl, whisk the olive oil with the pimentón.

2. Using a sharp paring knife, slice each potato crosswise at ⅛-inch intervals, cutting down but not all the way through the potato. Transfer the potatoes to a baking sheet. Drizzle with about ⅔ cup of the pimentón oil, season with salt and pepper and toss to coat. Roast the potatoes cut sides up for 20 minutes. Insert one bay leaf into each potato and roast for about 20 minutes longer, until the potatoes are golden, crisp and cooked through. Transfer the potatoes to a platter, discard the bay leaves, drizzle with the remaining 2 tablespoons of pimentón oil and serve.

—Kay Chun

CREAMED KALE

Active 40 min; Total 1 hr 15 min; Serves 12

3½ lbs. Tuscan kale, 4 leaves left whole, the rest stemmed and chopped

¼ cup plus 1 Tbsp. extra-virgin olive oil

Kosher salt and pepper

2 Tbsp. unsalted butter

2 white onions, finely chopped

1½ cups heavy cream

1 Tbsp. honey

1. Preheat the oven to 350°. On a large baking sheet, rub the whole kale leaves with 1 tablespoon of the olive oil and season with salt and pepper. Bake for about 15 minutes, until crispy. Let cool.

2. Meanwhile, in a large pot, melt the butter in the remaining ¼ cup of olive oil. Add the onions, season with salt and cook over moderately high heat, stirring occasionally, until softened and just starting to brown, 8 to 10 minutes. Add the chopped kale and cook, stirring occasionally, until wilted, about 5 minutes. Add the cream and honey and bring to a simmer. Cover and cook over moderate heat, stirring occasionally, until the kale is very tender and coated in a thick sauce, 35 to 40 minutes.

3. Transfer half of the creamed kale to a food processor and puree until nearly smooth. Stir the puree into the pot and season with salt and pepper. Transfer the creamed kale to a serving bowl. Top with the crispy kale leaves and serve. *—Tyler Florence*

Suggested Pairing

A peppery California Cabernet Sauvignon is a perfect match for the prime rib.

basics

PANTRY ESSENTIALS

Keeping certain ingredients on hand at all times will help you whip up flavorful weeknight meals even when you are pressed for time.

Oils (extra-virgin olive, vegetable, canola, sesame) Keep a variety of oils on hand for both cooking and for adding flavor.

Vinegars (apple cider, balsamic, red wine, rice, sherry)

APPLE CIDER VINEGAR It has lower acidity than a lot of other vinegars. When it's mixed with other ingredients, it has a more neutral tone than balsamic or lemon juice.

BALSAMIC VINEGAR As defined by strict DOP (Denominazione di Origine Protetta) codes, only two regions can produce Aceto Balsamico Tradizionale. While it's worth seeking out those with the designation, there are plenty of good non-DOP balsamic vinegars available. The finest are thick, tart and intense.

RED WINE VINEGAR Tuscan food tends to have a healthy amount of acidity, which is complemented by the fruity complexity of red wine vinegar.

RICE VINEGAR Japanese rice vinegar is used in marinades and sauces, its slight sourness providing balance in salty, umami-rich dishes.

SHERRY VINEGAR In Spain's Jerez de la Frontera, sherry vinegar is aged using a special blending process that mixes younger vinegars with older ones. The resulting nutty-accented vinegar is a great finishing drizzle that brightens beans, balances chorizo or adds complexity to soups.

Hot Sauces (Louisiana-style, Sriracha, Scotch bonnet pepper sauce)

LOUISIANA-STYLE Most of the hot sauces with which we are familiar—Tabasco, Crystal, Frank's RedHot, Trappey's—arose from the same formula: vinegar + chiles + salt, pureed, then fermented.

SRIRACHA This fiery, garlicky, slightly sweet Thai sauce has an almost ubiquitous appeal.

SCOTCH BONNET PEPPER SAUCE In the Caribbean, hot sauces are called "pepper sauces," and the Scotch bonnet chile is the star of the show. It is on the hotter side, clocking in at 100,000 to 350,000 Scoville units.

Fish Sauce It's sodium, a little sweet and a lot of umami. Think of it as a liquid form of anchovy: It's not great if you have a big fistful, but if you put a little in then the flavor of everything else pops.

Soy Sauce A standard addition to stir-fries and Chinese takeout, soy sauce is a great way to bring umami to the table. A little soy sauce goes a long way in flavoring marinades, brines and dipping sauces. Light soy sauce is the standard, soy sauce used in most recipes. Dark soy sauce is basically light soy sauce to which caramel or molasses has been added, giving it a slightly sweeter flavor, darker color and a thicker texture.

Capers, Cornichons and Pickles Add a distinctly briny, slightly sour flavor with a variety of pickles and dark green caper berries.

Tomato Paste, Puree and Whole Tomatoes Use canned tomatoes such as San Marzano to make quick tomato sauce with garlic and olive oil. They're not seasonal, so you can cook with them year-round.

HEAT

Horseradish

Hot pepper
sauce

Scotch bonnet
hot sauce

Urfa pepper

Sriracha

TANG

Cabernet
vinegar

Red wine
vinegar

Pickled
okra

Dill pickles

Cornichons

Mango
pickles

Indian mixed
pickles

Keralan
pickle puree

Dijon mustard

Canned Coconut Milk With its delicate tropical flavor and luscious texture, coconut milk remains a popular dairy alternative and a go-to pantry item for home cooks who love curries.

Tahini Whisk this with lemon juice and hot water to make a rich dressing that's wonderful on everything, especially roasted vegetables.

Kimchi Add to scrambled eggs or tacos. The brine makes a great cucumber salad dressing.

Stocks (beef, chicken, fish, vegetable) Stocks are basic ingredients for cooking and canned versions can help simplify recipes.

Nut Butters (almond butter, peanut butter) Nut butters are not just for sandwiches—use them to add nutty flavor to sauces, toppings, noodles and desserts.

Canned Beans (chickpeas, black, pinto) Canned beans are super-cheap, a great source of protein, and they're ready when you are.

Canned Tuna Packed in Oil Go beyond tuna salad and use this versatile pantry staple to make last-minute pasta sauces or a pâté.

Anchovies Packed in Oil According to chef José Andrés, the best anchoas in the world are caught in the Cantabrian Sea between April and June, cured in salt and preserved in extra-virgin olive oil.

Mustard (Dijon, grainy) Yellow mustard is fine for barbecues, but for cooking, you need something better. Whisk Dijon into vinaigrettes or use to season chicken, pork, or fish.

Dried Fruit (cherries and golden raisins) Drying fruit helps to preserve it for a much longer time and concentrates its flavor and sweetness. Dried fruit goes especially well with meat and is included in many Mediterranean and Middle Eastern recipes.

Nuts (walnuts, almonds, pine nuts) Use nuts to add both flavor and texture to a variety of dishes including salads, main dishes and desserts. Roasting nuts brings out the flavor in nuts and creates a richer, more intense nutty taste.

Pasta Keep a variety of shapes and sizes of dried pasta on hand as pastas are fairly interchangeable if you substitute one that is a similar shape and size.

Rice (arborio, basmati, brown) Arborio is a medium-grain rice that's often used for risotto. Basmati is a long-grain rice known for its fragrance, and brown rice is hulled with the bran intact, giving this rice a chewy texture and nutty flavor.

Grains (barley, bulgur, quinoa) Versatile grains are easy to prepare and often provide a neutral background to highlight other ingredients.

Flours (all-purpose, almond, coconut, whole wheat)

ALMOND FLOUR A protein-rich flour that's often used in gluten-free and Paleo diet cooking, this flour adds healthy fat, moisture and nutty flavor.

COCONUT FLOUR Made from dried, defatted coconut meat, this flour is high in both protein and fiber and has a coconut flavor.

Panko Breadcrumbs
These Japanese breadcrumbs are made by coarsely shredding the tender inner portion of a loaf of bread instead of grinding the entire loaf to a powder. The results are extra crispy, light and sweet.

Sugar (granulated, confectioners', light and dark brown) Sugars vary in color and texture so keep several on hand for use in different types of recipes.

Spices (crushed red pepper, ancho chili powder, pimentón de la Vera, turmeric)

PIMENTÓN DE LA VERA Chef José Andrés calls this sweet smoked Spanish paprika a must-have.

TURMERIC This peppery spice adds flavor and color to curries but can be used in a wide variety of dishes.

Bittersweet and Semisweet Chocolate These terms are often used interchangeably since there is no official distinction. Generally, bittersweet is less sweet than semisweet but both are commonly used in baking.

KEY RECIPES

A few key recipes can be the foundation for flavorful meals. When you keep homemade basics like vinaigrette, pesto, tomato sauce, hot sauce, stocks, hummus and Greek yogurt on hand, you're one step closer to dinner.

BASIC VINAIGRETTE

Total 5 min; Makes 1 cup

3 Tbsp. red wine vinegar

1 garlic clove, minced

1 tsp. Dijon mustard

Kosher salt and pepper

¾ cup extra-virgin olive oil

In a pint-size jar, combine the red wine vinegar, garlic, Dijon mustard, ¾ teaspoon salt and ½ teaspoon pepper. Cover and shake to dissolve the salt. Add the olive oil and shake to blend. —*Hugh Acheson*

MAKE AHEAD Vinaigrette can be refrigerated in an airtight container for 2 weeks.

GREEK VARIATION Add 1 teaspoon chopped oregano and ½ teaspoon finely grated lemon zest.

DILL PICKLE VARIATION Puree with 1 chopped large kosher dill pickle.

MISO VARIATION Add 1 tablespoon white miso paste.

FRENCH-STYLE VARIATION Add 1 teaspoon chopped tarragon.

SPICY SESAME VARIATION Add 1 tablespoon toasted sesame seeds, 1 tablespoon toasted sesame oil and 1 teaspoon crushed red pepper.

KIMCHI VARIATION Add 2 tablespoons finely chopped cabbage kimchi.

GINGER VARIATION Add 2 tablespoons minced peeled fresh ginger.

BASIL PESTO

Total 10 min; Makes ¾ cup

¼ cup extra-virgin olive oil, plus more for brushing

¼ cup pine nuts

2 garlic cloves, smashed

¼ cup freshly grated Parmesan cheese

2 cups (lightly packed) basil leaves

½ tsp. fresh lemon juice

Salt

1. Brush a small skillet with olive oil and heat over moderately high heat. Add the pine nuts and toast, stirring constantly, until golden, about 3 minutes. Transfer to a plate to cool.

2. In a food processor or blender, pulse the pine nuts with the garlic and Parmesan until finely chopped. Add the basil and pulse until minced, scraping down the side of the bowl. With the machine on, add the ¼ cup of olive oil in a thin stream and process until smooth. Add the lemon juice and season with salt. —*Tim McKee*

MAKE AHEAD The pesto can be refrigerated overnight; press a piece of plastic wrap directly on the surface to keep the pesto from discoloring.

TOMATO SAUCE

Active 15 min; Total 1 hr; Makes 3 cups

2 Tbsp. extra-virgin olive oil

1 small white onion, finely chopped

1 medium carrot, grated

One 28-oz. can whole plum tomatoes in juice, coarsely pureed

Kosher salt

1 Tbsp. unsalted butter

2 tsp. finely chopped oregano

In a medium saucepan, heat the olive oil over moderate heat until shimmering. Add the onion and cook, stirring, until softened, about 8 minutes. Stir in the carrot, then add the tomatoes and season with salt. Simmer over moderately low heat, stirring occasionally, until the sauce has thickened, about 40 minutes. Remove from the heat and stir in the butter and oregano. —*Hugh Acheson*

LOUISIANA HOT SAUCE
Active 15 min; Total 35 min; Makes about 1 pint

2 cups water

10 oz. fresh hot red chiles such as tabasco, cayenne or serrano

1 small onion, chopped

3 garlic cloves, finely chopped

Kosher salt

1 cup distilled white vinegar

1. In a medium saucepan, bring the water, chiles, onion, garlic and 1 teaspoon salt to a boil. Reduce the heat and simmer until the vegetables are very tender, 15 to 20 minutes.

2. Let the mixture cool to warm, then puree in a blender with the vinegar. Season with salt to taste, then place in a pint jar. Refrigerate for at least 3 weeks for optimal flavor. —*Ian Knauer*

MAKE AHEAD The hot sauce keeps refrigerated for at least 9 months.

JAMAICAN HOT SAUCE
Active 30 min; Total 45 min; Makes about 1 quart

12 oz. red, orange or yellow Scotch bonnet chiles

1 bunch scallion whites, trimmed

2¼ cups distilled white vinegar

2 Tbsp. dark brown sugar

¼ tsp. ground allspice

Kosher salt

1. In a food processor, pulse the chiles and scallion whites until finely chopped.

2. In a medium saucepan, bring the vinegar, brown sugar, allspice and 2 tablespoons salt to a simmer, stirring to dissolve the sugar. Add the chile mixture to the saucepan and bring to a simmer. Simmer 1 minute, then remove from the heat and let cool. Store in jars in the refrigerator. —*Ian Knauer*

JE HOT SAUCE
Active 30 min; Total 5 hr 30 min; Makes 3½ cups

4 cups extra-virgin olive oil

1 large onion, cut into 2-inch pieces

1 large tomato, cut into 2-inch pieces

1 red bell pepper, seeded and cut into 2-inch pieces

1 Cubanelle pepper, seeded and cut into 2-inch pieces

9 serrano chiles, stemmed

7 garlic cloves

5 habanero chiles, stemmed

Kosher salt

1. In a large saucepan, combine all of the ingredients except the salt. Cook over low heat until all of the vegetables are falling-apart soft, about 4 hours; let cool slightly.

2. Drain the vegetables in a fine sieve set over a heatproof bowl, reserving 2 cups of the cooking oil; don't press on the solids. Transfer the vegetables to a blender, add ¼ cup of water and pulse until finely chopped. With the machine on, gradually drizzle in 2 cups of the reserved cooking oil and puree until smooth and slightly thick. Season with salt and let cool completely before serving. —*Jose Enrique*

MAKE AHEAD The hot sauce can be refrigerated for up to 2 weeks.

Chicken Stock

CHICKEN STOCK

Active 30 min; Total 8 hr 30 min; Makes 3 quarts

Homemade stock is a beautiful thing, infusing everything it touches with layers of flavor. Plus, it's ridiculously easy to make. Put the ingredients in a pot and walk away. It's the ultimate culinary mic drop.

One 3½- to 4-lb. chicken, quartered

2 medium-size white onions, quartered

3 large carrots, scrubbed and cut into 2-inch pieces

3 celery ribs with leaves, cut into 2-inch pieces

2 garlic cloves

2 parsley sprigs

2 thyme sprigs

2 bay leaves

1 tsp. coriander seeds

6 black peppercorns

Kosher salt

1. In a large stockpot, combine 4 quarts of water with all of the ingredients except the salt. Simmer over very low heat, partially covered, for 8 hours; skim the surface of the stock as necessary.

2. Strain the stock through a fine sieve into a large bowl and season with salt. Reserve the chicken for another use; discard remaining solids. Let the stock cool, then refrigerate. Skim the fat from the surface before using. —*Hugh Acheson*

MAKE AHEAD The stock can be refrigerated for up to 5 days or frozen for up to 1 month.

VEGETABLE SCRAP STOCK

Active 5 min; Total 45 min; Makes 3 cups

4 cups vegetable scraps (carrot peels, onion skins, herb stems, mushroom stems, etc.)

3 Tbsp. extra-virgin olive oil

Preheat the oven to 350°. In a medium bowl, toss the vegetable scraps with the olive oil. Spread on a rimmed baking sheet and roast for 10 minutes, or beginning to brown. Scrape into a stockpot and cover with 6 cups of water. Simmer until the liquid has reduced by half, about 30 minutes. Strain through a fine sieve set over a medium bowl; discard the solids. —*Jehangir Mehta*

RICH BEEF STOCK

Active 15 min; Total 6 hr 10 min; Makes 1½ quarts

1 tsp. vegetable oil

5 lbs. meaty beef shanks, cut into 2-inch pieces

2 large carrots, cut into 2-inch lengths

2 celery stalks, cut into 2-inch lengths

1 large onion, quartered

4 qt. water

Sea salt

1. Preheat the oven to 450°. Heat the oil in a large roasting pan set over 2 burners. Add the beef shanks and cook over moderate heat until sizzling and lightly browned on 1 side, about 5 minutes. Transfer the pan to the oven and roast for 45 minutes, or until the meat and bones are browned. Add the carrots, celery and onion and roast for about 30 minutes longer, or until the vegetables are lightly browned.

2. Scrape the meat, bones and vegetables into a stockpot. Set the roasting pan over high heat and add 1 cup of the water. Cook, scraping up the browned bits, until the pan is clean. Pour the pan juices into the stockpot along with the remaining 3 cups and 3 quarts of water and simmer over moderately high heat for 30 minutes, skimming occasionally. Reduce the heat to moderately low, cover partially and simmer until the stock is richly flavored and reduced to 2 quarts, about 4 hours. Season with salt.

3. Strain the stock through a fine sieve set over a heatproof bowl; discard the solids. Refrigerate until cold, scrape off the fat and discard. Before using, boil the stock until reduced to 6 cups. —*Grace Parisi*

MAKE AHEAD The stock can be refrigerated for 1 week or frozen for up to 2 months.

FISH STOCK

Active 10 min; Total 1 hr 20 min; Makes about 9 cups

½ cup extra-virgin olive oil

2 lbs. fish heads and bones, rinsed

1 leek, white and tender green parts only, thinly sliced

1 medium onion, finely chopped

1 fennel bulb, finely chopped

One 750-ml. bottle dry white wine

1 bunch parsley stems

Salt

In a large stockpot, heat the oil. Add the fish bones and the leek, onion and fennel and cook over moderately high heat, stirring, until the vegetables are just tender, 15 minutes. Add the wine and bring to a boil. Cook over moderately high heat until reduced by half, 20 minutes. Add 8 cups of water and the parsley stems and simmer over moderate heat for 30 minutes. Strain the broth through a fine mesh sieve set over a bowl and season lightly with salt. Discard the solids.

MAKE AHEAD The stock can be frozen for up to 2 months.

TAHINI SAUCE

Total 10 min; Makes 1¼ cups

½ cup tahini

1¼ Tbsp. fresh lemon juice

1 garlic clove, minced

1 Tbsp. finely chopped flat-leaf parsley

1 Tbsp. finely chopped mint

Salt

In a food processor, combine the tahini with the lemon juice and garlic. Add ¾ cup of water and puree until smooth. Transfer the sauce to a bowl and whisk in up to ½ cup more of water, until the sauce is pourable. Stir in the chopped parsley and mint, season with salt and serve.

MAKE AHEAD The tahini sauce can be refrigerated for up to 2 days.

ISRAELI HUMMUS WITH PAPRIKA AND WHOLE CHICKPEAS

Active 15 min; Total 1 hr 15 min plus overnight soaking
Makes 4 cups

½ lb. dried chickpeas

1 Tbsp. baking soda

7 large garlic cloves, unpeeled

½ cup extra-virgin olive oil, divided

½ cup tahini, at room temperature

¼ cup plus 1 Tbsp. fresh lemon juice

¼ tsp. ground cumin, plus more for garnish

Salt

Paprika, for garnish

¼ cup chopped parsley

Pita bread, for serving

1. In a medium bowl, cover the dried chickpeas with 2 inches of water and stir in the baking soda. Refrigerate the chickpeas overnight. Drain the chickpeas and rinse them under cold water.

2. In a medium saucepan, cover the chickpeas with 2 inches of fresh water. Add the garlic cloves and bring to a boil. Simmer over moderately low heat until the chickpeas are tender, about 40 minutes. Drain, reserving ½ cup plus 2 tablespoons of the cooking water and 2 tablespoons of the chickpeas. Rinse the remaining chickpeas under cold water. Peel the garlic cloves.

3. In a food processor, puree the chickpeas with ½ cup of the reserved cooking water, ¼ cup of the olive oil and 6 of the garlic cloves. Add ¼ cup each of the tahini and lemon juice and the cumin and process until creamy. Season the hummus with salt and transfer to a serving bowl.

4. Wipe out the food processor. Add the remaining ¼ cup of tahini, ¼ cup of olive oil, 2 tablespoons of reserved cooking water, 1 tablespoon of lemon juice and garlic clove and puree until creamy.

5. Using a ladle, make an indent in the center of the hummus. Spoon in the tahini-lemon mixture. Sprinkle the hummus with cumin and paprika. Garnish with reserved whole chickpeas and parsley and serve with pita bread.
—*Michael Solomonov*

BASIC HOMEMADE CORN TORTILLA

Total 30 min; Makes about 12 tortillas

2 cups masa harina

½ tsp. kosher or sea salt

1¼ to 1½ cups hot tap water

1. In a large bowl, combine the masa harina and salt. Start with 1¼ cups of water and mix into the masa mixture to form a semismooth dough ball. If necessary, add more water 1 tablespoon at a time until the dough binds together into a semismooth ball (dough should form easily into a ball but not be sticky). Knead 15 times or until the ball is smooth.

2. Pinch off 1-inch balls of dough. Form into tight balls, and then flatten into fat discs.

3. Between two sheets of plastic wrap, roll a dough ball to ⅛ inch thick by 6 inches in diameter (or press flat in a tortilla press).

4. Heat a griddle, comal (a smooth rounded griddle) or large skillet over medium heat. Place the raw tortilla on the pan and cook until it puffs and starts to brown, about 30 seconds, flip over, press down with a spatula, and then cook for another 30 seconds, or until the second side is browned.

5. Place the tortilla on a plate and cover with a towel. Repeat with the remaining dough balls.

—*Todd Porter and Diane Cru*

BASIC HOMEMADE FLOUR TORTILLA

Total 45 min; Makes about 12 tortillas

2 cups all-purpose flour

1 tsp. baking powder

1 tsp. kosher or sea salt

½ cup vegetable shortening or lard

¾ cup warm water

1. In a large bowl, whisk together the flour, baking powder and salt for 20 seconds. Pinch the vegetable shortening into the flour mixture or use a pastry cutter until incorporated. The mixture will be crumbly.

2. Start with ¾ cup of water and mix into the flour mixture to form a semismooth dough ball. If necessary, add more water 1 tablespoon at a time until dough binds together into a semismooth ball (dough should form easily into a ball but not be sticky). Knead 15 times or until the ball is smooth. Let the dough rest for 15 minutes.

3. Pinch off 1-inch balls of dough. Form into tight balls, and then flatten into fat discs. Allow to rest for 10 minutes.

4. Heat a griddle, comal (a smooth rounded griddle) or large skillet over medium heat. Place the raw tortilla on the pan and cook until it puffs and starts to brown, about 30 seconds, flip over, press down with a spatula, and then cook for another 30 seconds, or until the second side is browned.

5. Place the tortilla on a plate and cover with a towel. Repeat with the remaining dough balls.

—*Todd Porter and Diane Cru*

GREEK-STYLE YOGURT
Active 30 min; Total 7 hr plus overnight chilling
Makes about 2 quarts

1 gallon fat-free or 2 percent milk, preferably not ultrapasteurized

2 cups nonfat or 2 percent Greek-style plain yogurt with active cultures, at room temperature, or ¼ tsp. powdered yogurt culture (see Note)

1. In a large saucepan, bring 1½ inches of water to a boil. Set a large stainless steel bowl over the saucepan and add the milk; do not let the bowl touch the water. Turn the heat to low and gradually heat the milk, whisking, until it registers 180° on a candy thermometer. Keep the milk at 180° for 30 minutes, adjusting the heat as necessary.

2. Remove the bowl from the saucepan and let the milk cool down to 106°, stirring often. Meanwhile, preheat the oven to 110°. If using yogurt, whisk it with 2 cups of the warm milk in a bowl until smooth, then add it back into the warm milk. If using powdered yogurt culture, sprinkle the powder all over the warm milk.

3. Whisk the cultured warm milk for 3 minutes. Fill several clean jars to 1 inch below the rim with the cultured milk. Cap the jars and place in the warmed oven (or a yogurt maker or other gently heated spot); the cultured milk should stay between 105° and 110° during the entire process. Begin checking the yogurt after 4½ hours; it's ready when it is thick, tangy and surrounded by a small amount of clear whey. If using a pH meter, the yogurt is ready when it registers 4.5. Depending on how active the cultures are, it can take up to 18 hours for the yogurt to set and develop its characteristic tang. Refrigerate until thoroughly chilled or overnight.

4. Line a large colander or fine sieve with a moistened cotton cloth or several layers of cheesecloth and set it over a large bowl. Scoop the yogurt into the colander. Cover with plastic wrap and refrigerate for about 6 hours, or until it reaches the desired thickness.

MAKE AHEAD The strained yogurt can be refrigerated for up to 3 weeks.

NOTE Powdered yogurt culture can be ordered at culturesforhealth.com.

ALMOND MILK
Active 20 min; Total 1 hr 30 min plus overnight soaking
Makes 3 cups

1 cup raw almonds

5 cups filtered water, plus more for soaking

4 plump Medjool dates, pitted

¼ tsp. ground cinnamon

Sea salt

1. In a medium bowl, cover the almonds with filtered water and let stand overnight at room temperature.

2. Drain and rinse the almonds; transfer to a blender. Add the dates, cinnamon, 5 cups of water and 2 pinches of salt to the blender and puree on high speed until very smooth, about 2 minutes. Pour the nut milk through a cheesecloth-lined fine sieve set over a bowl and let drain for 30 minutes. Using a spatula, press on the solids to extract any remaining milk; discard the solids. Transfer the nut milk to an airtight container and refrigerate until chilled, about 30 minutes. Stir or shake before serving.
—*Teresa Piro*

MAKE AHEAD The almond milk can be refrigerated for up to 4 days.

NOTE You can use the leftover ground nuts in baked goods or smoothies. After making nut milk, spread the nuts out on a rimmed baking sheet in an even layer and bake at 200° until pale and dry, about 2 hours. Let cool completely, then pulse in a food processor until fine crumbs form.

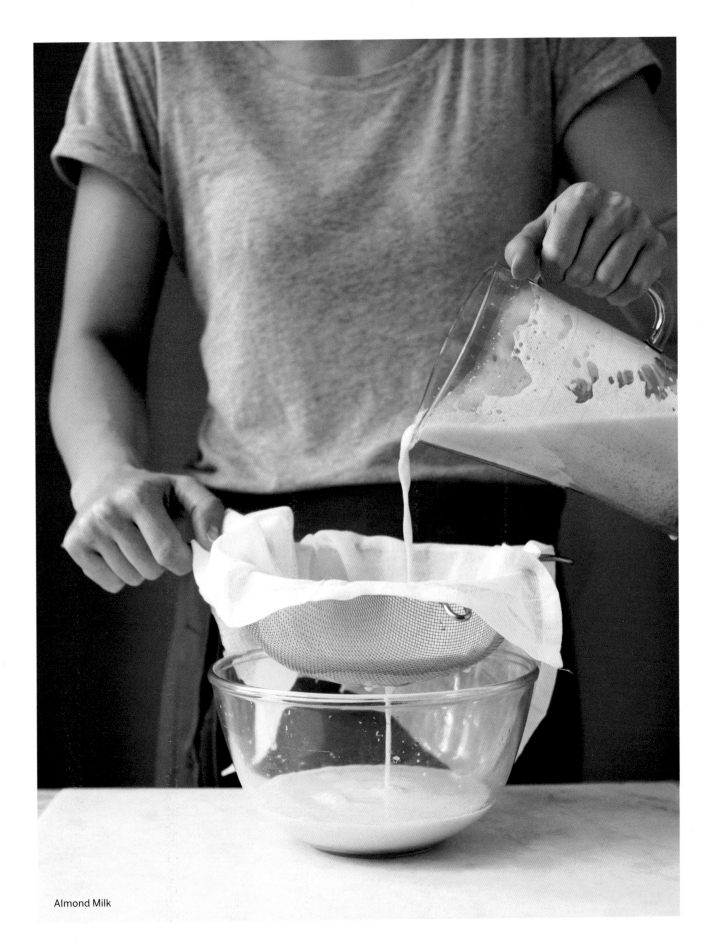

Almond Milk

SMART IDEAS FOR LEFTOVERS

Chefs face the same quandary you do on weekday nights: what to cook with a fridge full of extra ingredients and leftovers. Curb food waste in your kitchen with these smart and delicious ideas for transforming scraps and leftovers into tasty dishes.

PASTA

Baked pasta

"When leftover baked pasta is firm and cold, scoop it with a large spoon or ice cream scoop, and shape it into balls with your hands. Roll them in flour, then egg wash and then panko breadcrumbs. Deep-fry them in peanut or canola oil and devour. These fantastic arancini are a weeknight wonder dish." —Abbi Adams

Mac and cheese

"What I like to do is take the giant, solid block that cold macaroni and cheese becomes after you've refrigerated it overnight, slice it, put a bunch more cheddar cheese on it and broil the hell out of it. It gets really crispy and gooey on the outside but super melty on the inside. It's not transforming it so much as giving it a new crispy edge, which is my favorite part." —Grae Nonas

FISH

Grilled salmon

Wrap leftover grilled salmon in tortillas and top with cabbage, cilantro, radishes and sour cream or pickled onions and lentils for tacos.

Dress leftover salmon with herby yogurt and stuff the salad in a hot dog bun for a salmon roll.

POULTRY

Turkey and gravy

Whisk gravy into hot water or canned chicken broth for a soup base, then stir in diced turkey.

Grilled chicken

Use shredded chicken as a filling for fast, easy tacos. "I'm not English at all, but bubble and squeak is seriously the most genius form of leftovers of all time. We take all the vegetables from a roasted chicken and mix them all together with leftover mashed potatoes. We make little patties, panfry them and put poached eggs on top. Don't forget the bacon." —Daniel Jacobs

Roast chicken

"Leftover roast chicken is great in a quinoa salad. I make Spanish omelettes with leftover vegetables, and tortillas stuffed with deboned buffalo wings. I could go on all day." —Jamie Bissonette

BEEF AND LAMB

Roast beef

For steak sandwiches, fry thin slices of beef in a skillet and arrange them on a baguette. Top with sautéed onions and cheese, and toast under the broiler until the cheese melts.

To make a smoky beef-and-bean chili, cut roast beef into 1-inch pieces, then combine with your favorite mix of beans, vegetables and smoked paprika.

Braised meats

Make ragùs with extra short ribs and serve over pasta or polenta.

Meatballs

Turn leftover meatballs into a pizza. Mash meatballs into tomato sauce, then spread on parbaked pizza dough and bake for 10 minutes.

For a simple casserole, use leftover meatballs and an Italian-style tomato sauce, spread in a baking dish, add cooked pasta, then cover with a melty cheese like Fontina. Bake until sauce is bubbling and cheese is browned.

Leg of lamb

Stuff lamb, pickled red onions, feta cheese and a tomato-ginger compote into pita pockets for a quick sandwich. Use tender, juicy lamb in quesadillas—and serve with a tangy cucumber-yogurt sauce.

BREAD

Stale bread

"Make a seasonal panzanella (bread salad) or fry up small pieces of bread in butter to make toasted breadcrumbs." —Travis McShane

"Grind bread with a mortar and pestle with garlic, almonds and hazelnuts to make pesto for chicken or fish." —Alex Figura

"Toast leftover bread and crush it up to use as a thickening agent in a sauce, soup or mole." —Kaelin Ulrich Trilling

"Rip up leftover bread and throw it into a veggie frittata." —Lachlan McKinnon-Patterson

CHEESE

Leftover cheese

At the end of their wine-and-cheese parties, cheese-whizzes Helen Jane Hearn and Natalie Wassum gather any leftovers to make an incredible mac and cheese later in the week. Make an awesome leftover cheese fondue and use leftover bread and roasted potatoes for dipping.

VEGETABLES, HERBS AND FRUITS

Vegetable scraps

Store broccoli stems, carrot butts and other extra vegetable scraps in zip-top bags and use them for slaws and stocks.

Mushroom stems

"Simmer mushroom stems with dashi and miso, then puree into a soup." —*Andrew Carmellini*

Vegetable stems

"I like to slice the stems from raw greens and herbs really thin (think chives) and use them like an herb to give some added flavor, freshness, and crunch to salads." —*Josh Habiger*

"Cut the stems of greens very small and then reduce them with white wine, sugar and tomatoes to make a jam." —*Kaelin Ulrich Trilling*

Brussels sprout nubs

"Use Brussels sprout nubs to make a slaw or kraut." —*Richard Blais*

Carrot tops

"Look at your carrot and turnip tops and think pesto. Or soup." —*Dan Barber*

Root vegetable peels

"Use root vegetable peels mixed with cheese (Gouda, Parmesan, anything hard) to make a ravioli filling. Make it even easier by using wonton skins as pasta sheets." —*Paul Reilly*

Leek greens

Chef Mohammad Islam pickles leek greens and tosses them into lobster pasta to add tanginess and texture.

Garlic skins

Chef Alex Figura saves garlic skins and uses them to infuse oil or butter.

Potato peels

Save the potato peels for a Spanish-style tortilla or Parmigiano-Reggiano cheese puffs.

"Just fry those bad boys up and make poutine." —*Josh Munchel*

Mashed potatoes

Whip mashed potatoes and grated cheddar into hot stock for a creamy, thick soup.

Mashed potatoes can be the basis for excellent potato pancakes: Mix them with egg, flour and salt and panfry until crisp.

Roasted potatoes

For a hash, sauté some onions and chiles, then add leftover roasted potatoes and cook until warm. Top with fried eggs before serving.

For a simple side dish, cook tough greens like kale or chard, then add the leftover roasted potatoes and heat until warm. Sprinkle with crumbled bacon, if desired.

Herb stems

"Put herb stems in a blender with a little jalapeño, orange and fresh herbs and blend together to make a marinade or herb broth that can be used to cook mussels or to brighten up cooked grains." —*Travis McShane*

"Take all of your leftover herb stems and put them into a bottle of white wine vinegar (or whichever vinegar you like) and let them sit there for as long as you want. It will give your vinegar some depth and personality." —*Josh Habiger*

Citrus rinds

"Blanch lemon, lime or orange rinds five to seven times, then blend with simple syrup to create a dairy-free citrus cream." —*Alex Figura*

Citrus peels

"Citrus peels never go to waste at our restaurant. Whenever we juice a citrus fruit, we first zest the peel with a Microplane and make citrus salts for seasoning fish and meat, or we dry the zest to flavor cakes and ice creams." —*Ryan Brazeal*

Apples

They might be too mushy to eat raw, but bruised apples are great in a rich, sweet applesauce.

index

C

CABBAGE
Apple Cider–Braised Cabbage, 206
Red-and-Green Coleslaw, 218
Slow Cooker Corned Beef with Cabbage, Carrots and Potatoes, 60
Cake, Fallen Olive Oil Soufflé, 172
Caperberries and Charred Lemons, Chicken Roasted on Bread with, 201

CAPERS
Sautéed Chicken with Olives, Capers and Roasted Lemons, 136
Caramel, Coconut Crème, 83

CARROTS
Carrot and Daikon Pickles, 103
Chipotle-Roasted Baby Carrots, 160
Curry-Roasted Carrots with Carrot Top Gremolata, 202
Minty Peas and Carrots, 156
Sautéed Carrots with Lemon and Marjoram, 182
Slow Cooker Corned Beef with Cabbage, Carrots and Potatoes, 60
Cashews, Grilled Fig Salad with Spiced, 128
Cauliflower Puree with Horseradish and Caraway, 36
Cazuela, Creamy Tuna Noodle, 73
Celery, Fennel and Apple Salad with Pecorino and Walnuts, 194
Celery Root with Goat Butter, Roasted Beets and, 206

CHEESE
Andouille Mac & Cheese, 209
Buttermilk-Parmesan Biscuits, 52
Celery, Fennel and Apple Salad with Pecorino and Walnuts, 194
Cheese Enchiladas with Red Chile Sauce, 19
Celery, Fennel, and Apple Salad with Pecorino and Walnuts, 194
Corn on the Cob with Parsley Butter and Parmesan, 117
Feta-and-Radish Toasts, 190
Fresh Cheese Spaetzle, 148
Gruyère Cheese Soufflé, 181
Herbed Zucchini-Feta Fritters, 70
Little Gem Lettuce with Roasted Beets and Feta Dressing, 16
Oven Fries with Herbs and Pecorino, 140
Pumpkin Layer Cake with Mascarpone Frosting, 234
Rigatoni All'Amatriciana, 151

Roasted Brussels Sprout and Gruyère Quiche, 177
Rustic Sausage and Three-Cheese Lasagna, 214
Spinach, Feta and Tarragon Frittata, 15
Squash Gratin, 124
Tomato-Feta Salad with Lime and Mint, 118
Tomato Soup with Feta, Olives and Cucumbers, 70
Watermelon, Feta and Charred Pepper Salad, 110

CHICKEN
Arroz Con Pollo, 89
Chicken Roasted on Bread with Caperberries and Charred Lemons, 201
Chicken Stock, 236
Chipotle Chicken Tacos, 85
Gingery Chicken Satay with Peanut Sauce, 82
Lemon-Thyme Roast Chicken, 143
Sautéed Chicken with Olives, Capers and Roasted Lemons, 136
Soy-Maple-Glazed Chicken Legs, 48
Spicy Green Posole, 197

CHICKPEAS
Chickpea Vegetable Stew, 189
Israeli Hummus with Paprika and Whole Chickpeas, 238

CHILES
Cheese Enchiladas with Red Chile Sauce, 19
Chipotle Chicken Tacos, 85
Chipotle-Roasted Baby Carrots, 160
Fish Tacos with Tomatillo-Jalapeño Salsa, 31
Grilled Vegetables with Roasted-Chile Butter, 86
Je Hot Sauce, 235
Louisiana Hot Sauce, 235
Salmon, Broccolini and Fresh Red Chile Papillotes, 43
Sausage Burgers with Grilled Green Chiles, 97
Smoked-Chile-and-Mango Guacamole, 86
Spicy Dill Quick Pickles, 140
Spicy Green Posole, 197
Sriracha-Roasted Broccoli, 48
Tacos al Pastor, 159
Tequila-Chipotle Shrimp, 27
Chili, Cumin, 186
Chips, Baked Sweet Potato, 94

CHOCOLATE
Chocolate-Raspberry Truffletini, 215
Creamy Mocha Ice Pops, 94
Double-Chocolate Cookie Crumble, 187
Hazelnut Chocolate Bars, 218

COCONUT
Coconut Crème Caramel, 83
Coconut Jasmine Rice, 83
Warm Lentil and Root Vegetable Salad with Coconut Tzatziki, 190
Coleslaw, Red-and-Green, 218

CORN
Corn on the Cob with Parsley Butter and Parmesan, 117
Corn on the Cob with Seasoned Salts, 98
Skillet Corn and Peppers with Cilantro-Lime Mayo, 20
Crab Cakes, Baltimore-Style, 40
Cranberry Gingerbread, 148
Crudités à la Mexicaine, 20

CUCUMBERS
Cucumber–Sugar Snap Salad, 94
Pork Schnitzel with Cucumber Salad, 147
Spicy Dill Quick Pickles, 140
Taiwanese Sesame Cucumbers, 83
Tomato Soup with Feta, Olives and Cucumbers, 70
Cumin Chili, 186

D

Daikon Pickles, Carrot and, 103
Dandelion Greens Salsa Verde, Steamed New Potatoes with, 64

DATES
Almond Milk, 240
Quinoa Pilaf with Dates, Olives and Arugula, 24

DESSERTS
Coconut Crème Caramel, 83
Cranberry Gingerbread, 148
Creamy Mocha Ice Pops, 94
Double-Chocolate Cookie Crumble, 187
Fallen Olive Oil Soufflé Cake, 172
Grilled Fruit with Honeyed Lemon Thyme Vinegar, 118
Hazelnut Chocolate Bars, 218

Thin Grilled Lamb Chops with Lemon,
page 117; Corn on the Cob with Parsley
Butter and Parmesan, page 117

S

PHOTO CONTRIBUTORS

ANTONIO ACHILLEOS 53
CEDRIC ANGELES 107, 208
MATT ARMEDARIS 52
QUENTIN BACON 34, 104, 207
PAUL COSTELLO 64
CHRIS COURT 20, 65, 94,
DIANE CU 164, 199
JOHN CULLEN 28
HELENE DUJARDIN 33
PETER FRANK EDWARDS 106
ANNE FABER 132
EMILY FARRIS
TARA FISHER 228, 241
BROOK FITTS 198
PARKER FITZGERALD 124
SARA FORTE 182
NICOLE FRANZEN 66, 116, 119, 138, 220, 250
SCOTT HOCKER 25
ABBY HOCKING 45
CHRISTINA HOLMES 84, 122, 126, 129, 133, 161, 180, 183, 200, 219, 224, 226
JOHN KERNICK 9, 30, 57, 71, 95, 98, 110, 146, 153, 174, 191, 192, 196, 202, 203, 206, 227, 236, 246
EVA KOLENKO 3, 10, 12, 36, 42, 50, 120
SABRA KROCK 210
JONATHAN LOVEKIN 68, 114
JOHNNY MILLER 44, 72
MARCUS NILSSON 54, 111, 144
TODD PORTER 164, 199
CON POULOS FRONT COVER, 2, 7, 8, 14, 16, 17, 22, 29, 32, 37, 38, 46, 47, 49, 58, 59, 62, 75, 76, 80, 81, 87, 88, 91, 92, 99, 100, 101, 108, 112, 115, 128, 130, 135, 137, 142, 149, 150, 154, 155, 158, 165, 166, 167, 170, 176, 179, 184, 185, 204, 211, 212, 216, 242, BACK COVER
ANDREW PURSELL 194, 223
TINA RUPP 24, 96, 140, 173, 222
LUCY SCHAEFFER 26, 79, 86
FREDRIKA STJÄRNE 4, 11, 18, 21, 56, 141, 162, 188, 195, 230, 231, 233, 245, 256
JONNY VALIANT 145
ANNA WILLIAMS 74

CONVERSION CHART

BASIC MEASUREMENTS

GALLON	QUART	PINT	CUP	OUNCE	TBSP	TSP	DROPS
1 gal	4 qt	8 pt	16 c	128 fl oz			
½ gal	2 qt	4 pt	8 c	64 fl oz			
¼ gal	1 qt	2 pt	4 c	32 fl oz			
	½ qt	1 pt	2 c	16 fl oz			
	¼ qt	½ pt	1 c	8 fl oz	16 Tbsp		
			⅞ c	7 fl oz	14 Tbsp		
			¾ c	6 fl oz	12 Tbsp		
			⅔ c	5⅓ fl oz	10⅔ Tbsp		
			⅝ c	5 fl oz	10 Tbsp		
			½ c	4 fl oz	8 Tbsp		
			⅜ c	3 fl oz	6 Tbsp		
			⅓ c	2⅔ fl oz	5⅓ Tbsp	16 tsp	
			¼ c	2 fl oz	4 Tbsp	12 tsp	
			⅛ c	1 fl oz	2 Tbsp	6 tsp	
				½ fl oz	1 Tbsp	3 tsp	
					½ Tbsp	1½ tsp	
						1 tsp	60 drops
						½ tsp	30 drops

US TO METRIC CONVERSIONS

The conversions shown here are approximations. For more precise conversions, use the formulas to the right.

VOLUME

1 tsp	=	5 mL
1 Tbsp	=	15 mL
1 fl oz	=	30 mL
¼ c	=	59 mL
½ c	=	118 mL
¾ c	=	177 mL
1 c	=	237 mL
1 pt	=	½ L
1 qt	=	1 L
1 gal	=	4.4 L

WEIGHT

1 oz	=	28 g
¼ lb (4 oz)	=	113 g
½ lb (8 oz)	=	227 g
¾ lb (12 oz)	=	340 g
1 lb (16 oz)	=	½ kg

LENGTH

1 in	=	2.5 cm
5 in	=	12.7 cm
9 in	=	23 cm

TEMPERATURE

475°F	=	246°C
450°F	=	232°C
425°F	=	218°C
400°F	=	204°C
375°F	=	191°C
350°F	=	177°C
325°F	=	163°C
300°F	=	149°C
275°F	=	135°C
250°F	=	121°C

CONVERSION FORMULAS

$tsp \times 4.929 = mL$

$Tbsp \times 14.787 = mL$

$fl\ oz \times 29.574 = mL$

$c \times 236.588 = mL$

$pt \times 0.473 = L$

$qt \times 0.946 = L$

$oz \times 28.35 = g$

$lb \times 0.453 = kg$

$in \times 2.54 = cm$

$(°F - 32) \times 0.556 = °C$

More books from
FOOD&WINE

Perfect Pairings

With chapters arranged by the most popular grape varieties, this collection of classic recipes takes the guesswork out of what dish to serve with your favorite wines. The easy-to-follow wine primers break down the nuances of grape varieties and regions so you can shop for bottles like a pro.

Master Recipes

An intrepid cook's guide to dishes you've only ever dreamed about making at home, this must-have manual breaks down the best way to DIY everything from beef jerky to babka. With step-by-step instructions and photos, experts share their foolproof methods for over 180 delicious dishes. Along the way, you'll learn indispensable skills like fermenting pickles, making bread and tempering chocolate.

Mad Genius Tips

Did you know that you can poach a dozen eggs in a muffin tin? Or grate ginger with a fork? Or ripen bananas in the oven? Discover clever shortcuts and unexpected uses for everyday tools in a book that's as helpful as it is entertaining. Justin Chapple, the star of FOOD & WINE's Mad Genius Tips video series, shares more than 90 hacks for 100+ easy, fun and delicious recipes.